STEM
Lessons & Challenges
GRADE 1

The following illustrations were created by the artists listed (provided through Shutterstock.com) and are protected by copyright: Artur Balytskyi (pages 3-128); Altanaka, gladcov, Joy Brown (page 11); denk creative (pages 12, 20, 28, 36, 44, 52, 60, 68, 76, 84, 92, 100, 108, 116, 124); mhatzapa (pages 14-16, 22-24, 30-32, 35, 38-40, 46-48, 54-56, 62-64, 70-72, 78-80, 86-88, 94-96, 102-104, 110-112, 118-120, 126-128); Olgastocker (pages 14, 22, 30, 38, 46, 54, 62, 70, 78, 86, 94, 102, 110, 118, 126); Sopotnicki (page 19); Alexandra Giese (page 19); Naeblys, S-F, ziggy_mars (page 27); Ilikestudio, Infinity32829, JM-Design, Robyn Mackenzie, Waraporn Chokchaiworarat (page 35); Andrew McDonough, Frank Oppermann, Lenar Musin, robypangy (page 43); Alexander_P (page 51); Africa Studio, Luisa Leal Photography, Tim UR, varuna, Will Thomass, wk1003mike (page 59); shopplaywood (page 67); gst (page 75); Sundra (page 83); Andrew Lundquist, Dmitry Kalinovsky, Oleg Mikhaylov, Sergey Novikov (page 91); David M. Roberts, Farion_O, Polarpx, tony mills (page 99); Attphotography, Chaistock, Chris Godfrey, Eric Isselee, irin-k, Mila Supinskaya, Glashchenko, Nudchanat junsang (page 107); AlexGreenArt, K.A.Willis, Kjuuurs (page 115); Alta Oosthuizen, Anna Chudinovskykh, HelloRF Zcool, Joe Besure, Muellek Josef, WARUT MITTHUMSIRI, ZoranOrcik (page 123)

Writing: Tiffany Rivera
Content Editing: Kathleen Jorgensen
Lisa Vitarisi Mathews
Copy Editing: Laurie Westrich
Art Direction: Yuki Meyer
Illustration: Kris Sexton
Cover Design: Yuki Meyer
Design/Production: Paula Acojido
Yuki Meyer
Jessica Onken

EMC 9941

Evan-Moor
Helping Children Learn

Visit
teaching-standards.com
to view a correlation
of this book.
This is a free service.

Correlated to Current Standards

Congratulations on your purchase of some of the finest teaching materials in the world.

Photocopying the pages in this book is permitted for single-classroom use only. Making photocopies for additional classes or schools is prohibited.

For information about other Evan-Moor products, call 1-800-777-4362, fax 1-800-777-4332, or visit our website, www.evan-moor.com.
Entire contents © 2019 EVAN-MOOR CORP.
18 Lower Ragsdale Drive, Monterey, CA 93940-5746. Printed in USA.

CPSIA: Printed by McNaughton & Gunn, Saline, MI USA. [1/2019]

CONTENTS

What's in *STEM Lessons and Challenges* 4
How to Make STEM Challenges Successful 6
Why STEM Is Important 7
Tips for STEM Challenges 7
Request for Materials Form 8

Earth Science Challenges   Science Concept
Making Shade   Sunlight and Shadows 9
Natural Homes   Natural Resources 17

Physical Science Challenges   Science Concept
Tower   Structural Engineering (balance) 25
Maraca Music   Vibrations and Sound 33
Strong Roofs   Forces on Shapes 41
Telephone   Sound Waves 49
Soft Landing   Gravity and Energy 57
Bridge   Structural Engineering (stability) 65
Marble Roller Coaster   Force and Motion 73
Sailboat   Wind Power 81
Play Structures   Push and Pull Forces 89

Life Science Challenges   Science Concept
Bird Feeder   Animal Needs 97
Insect Catcher   Studying Insects 105
Joey Pouch   Adult Animals Caring for Offspring 113
Tool from Nature   Biomimicry 121

What's in *STEM Lessons and Challenges*

15 Engaging Units

Each grade of *STEM Lessons and Challenges* offers 15 grade-appropriate challenges representing life, earth, and physical science. Each unit is focused on a hands-on activity in which students work together as engineers to design, prototype, test, and refine their creation. Each unit also includes informational text and graphics about the science concepts at the core of the challenge.

Features

Teacher Overview
The unit begins with an overview that explains how to prepare students for the challenge and how students use the design process materials.

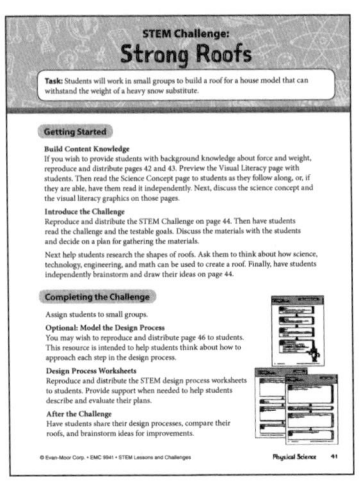

Science Concept and Visual Literacy
These pages provide students with foundational information about the concepts that are relevant to the challenge they are completing.

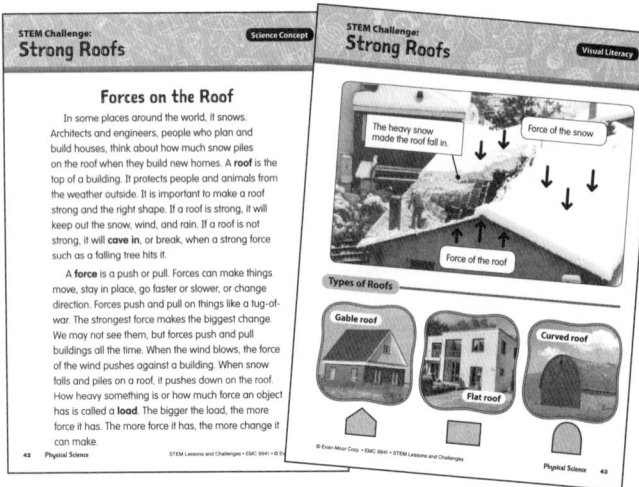

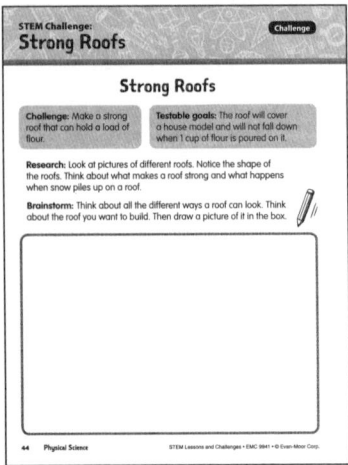

STEM Challenge
This page introduces students to the specific task and the goal(s). It also provides space for students to brainstorm their ideas individually.

STEM Lessons and Challenges • EMC 9941 • © Evan-Moor Corp.

Suggested Materials List

This unit-specific list is divided into two or three sections: items that each group should be given, items that should be available in a central location in the classroom for all groups to use, and items that relate specifically to testing whether each creation meets the goal. You may choose to substitute or add items as needed.

There are some items for testing that students should have access to while they are making their creations. These are listed in both the first and last sections. If the item is something that the teacher needs to make for each group, it will appear in a gray box in the first section.

Many of the materials are supplies that schools already have. If you need specific items, reproduce the letter to parents on page 8 and send it home with students.

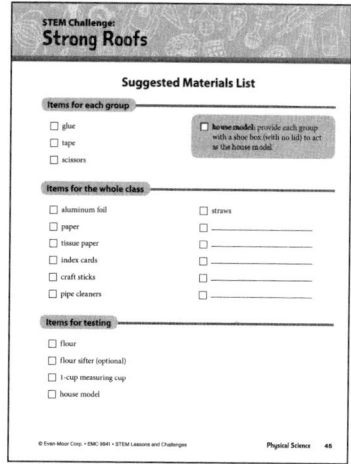

Think About the Design Process Worksheet

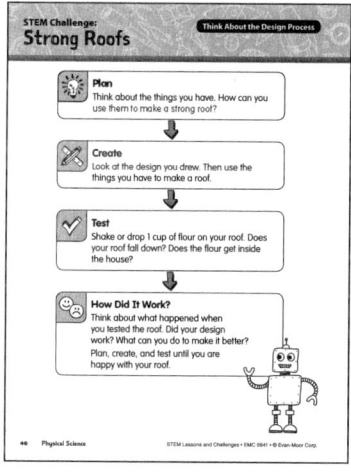

This optional page can be used to help students apply the design process to the specific unit.

Design Process and Redesign Process Worksheets

These worksheets guide students through each step of the design process and provide space to document their plan, materials, results, evaluations, and revisions.

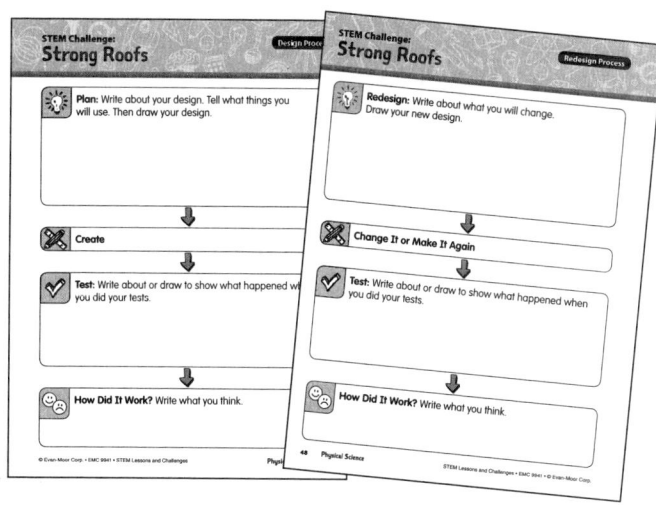

© Evan-Moor Corp. • EMC 9941 • STEM Lessons and Challenges

How to Make STEM Challenges Successful

- **Prepare for the lesson and the challenge.** Review the first page of the unit, which contains details for using each page of the unit. Also review the Suggested Materials List to see which materials you need for the challenge.

- **Determine the size of the groups students will work in.** Think about the materials needed, how long it will take to test their creations, and the optimal group size that encourages every student to be actively involved.

- **Determine the pace for completing the lesson and the challenge.** Plan how much time you will allot for students to read and discuss the Science Concept and Visual Literacy pages and to complete the individual and group brainstorming. The challenges can be created in a single time block. Some may require more than a day to dry, and some may require specific weather conditions in order to test the results.

- **Display the materials.** Allow students to see the available materials before they start to brainstorm. The materials may elicit ideas and also let them know what their constraints are.

- **Foster a creative environment.** Have students begin by brainstorming independently. This will allow students to work through their thought processes at their own pace. Once students are working in groups, let them design and problem-solve however they wish: sketch on paper, see how materials work together, or conceptualize in their head first. Remind students that there is no one correct solution.

- **Consider increasing the difficulty.** You may wish to set constraints, such as time limit, size, or minimum/maximum number of materials used.

- **Facilitate productive struggle.** Productive struggle is often part of the learning process. Guide students with leading questions if needed. Learning that occurs when students find and correct their own mistakes is strongest.

- **Support discussion and discourse.** Allow sufficient time for sharing solutions and results and discussing design strategies. Modeling a variety of approaches offers valuable learning benefits and encourages peer respect and cooperation.

- **Extend the lesson.** You can expand the activity to incorporate other content areas:
  - Have groups give their creation a brand name or design (art and economics).
  - Have groups create an ad for their creation (art and economics).
  - Give each material a dollar value and require groups to stick to a budget (math and economics).
  - Have groups summarize their stumbles and success and details of what they learned along the way (science and language arts).

Why STEM Is Important

Including STEM lessons in your curriculum is more important than ever. Economists say that by the middle of the century, there will be 80,000,000 new jobs in automation. Technology is growing at a tremendous rate. The students you are teaching now will be tomorrow's innovators. They will need to reason and be creative to solve problems that don't exist yet!

STEM projects integrate science, technology, engineering, and math skills in a problem-solving challenge. These hands-on challenges invite students to apply critical thinking, innovation, and communication to solve all types of real-world problems, even those in areas other than science or engineering.

The STEM projects in this book foster an innovator's mindset: an innovator is collaborative, observant, persistent, flexible, aware of others' needs, and unafraid to risk failure. There are many routes to solutions. Few are clear; most have dead ends along the way. Students learn much about what not to do from dead ends, which are as valuable as the more obvious successes. Even if students don't meet the original goal, what they have learned along the way makes the trip valuable.

The STEM projects should be attempted in groups. As in real jobs, people work in teams, contributing their unique perspective and ideas and learning from others. This fosters communication, collaboration, and respect for others.

Reproduce and distribute to students.

Tips for STEM Challenges

STEM challenges make your brain grow. There are many ways to do them. Be creative! These tips can help.

Think about all the ways to use the materials. You can use a straw in many ways. You can blow through it. It makes things roll. It holds things up. It floats.

Think about what you read and your goal. What you read is a clue to what you will create. Compare the examples with what you want to make.

Try different things. Put the materials together in different ways. See what they do. Then add something or change something.

Don't give up! It takes many tries to make a new thing. Learn from what doesn't work. When you figure it out, you'll feel great!

Reproduce and distribute to students.

STEM Materials Needed

Dear Parent/Guardian,

Our class is doing a STEM activity on _____.
(date)

Can you please provide the following materials by the date above?

_____   _____

_____   _____

Thank you!
Sincerely,

_____, Room _____

Reproduce and distribute to students.

STEM Materials Needed

Dear Parent/Guardian,

Our class is doing a STEM activity on _____.
(date)

Can you please provide the following materials by the date above?

_____   _____

_____   _____

Thank you!
Sincerely,

_____, Room _____

STEM Challenge: Making Shade

Task: Students will work in small groups to design a structure that provides shade for two small toys.

Getting Started

Build Content Knowledge
If you wish to provide students with background knowledge about sunlight, shadows, and shade, reproduce and distribute pages 10 and 11. Preview the Visual Literacy page with students. Then read the Science Concept page to students as they follow along, or, if they are able, have them read it independently. Next, discuss the science concept and the visual literacy graphics on those pages.

Introduce the Challenge
Reproduce and distribute the STEM Challenge on page 12. Then have students read the challenge and the testable goals. Discuss the materials with the students and decide on a plan for gathering the materials.

Next, help students research ways to protect themselves from sunlight. Ask them to think about how science, technology, engineering, and math can be used to create a structure that provides shade. Finally, have students independently brainstorm and draw their ideas on page 12.

Completing the Challenge

Assign students to small groups.

Optional: Model the Design Process
You may wish to reproduce and distribute page 14 to students. This resource is intended to help students think about how to approach each step in the design process.

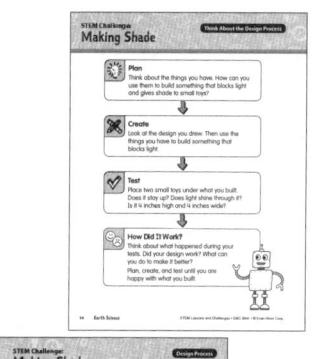

Design Process Worksheets
Reproduce and distribute the STEM design process worksheets to students. Provide support when needed to help students describe and evaluate their plans.

After the Challenge
Have students share their design processes, compare their shady structures, and brainstorm ideas for improvements.

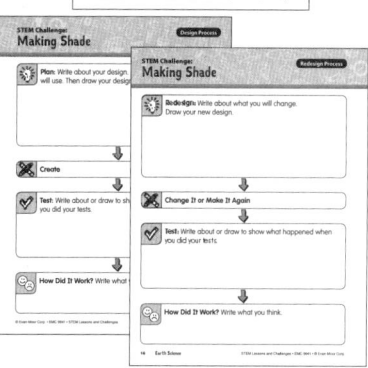

STEM Challenge: Making Shade

Science Concept

Shade from the Sun's Energy

The sun gives us light and energy that help us live and grow. We can see the energy as light. We can feel the energy as heat. But the sun's light and heat are powerful. Too much sunlight can hurt living things. It can hurt our eyes, burn our skin, and make us too hot. We must stay safe in the sun.

Light travels in a straight line. It can shine through some things, like a glass window or water. Light cannot shine through other things, like wood, a rock, or a ball. When light cannot move through something, you can see a **shadow**. A shadow is a dark shape that appears when an object blocks light. The darkness from the shadow is called **shade**. It helps keep you cool and safe from the sun's light.

A great place to find shade is under a tree. The branches and leaves of a tree grow out from the thick trunk. Light cannot shine through wood or leaves, so a shadow appears in the shape of the tree. You can also stand under an umbrella to get shade. The shade from a tree or an umbrella helps you stay safe on a sunny day.

STEM Challenge: Making Shade

Visual Literacy

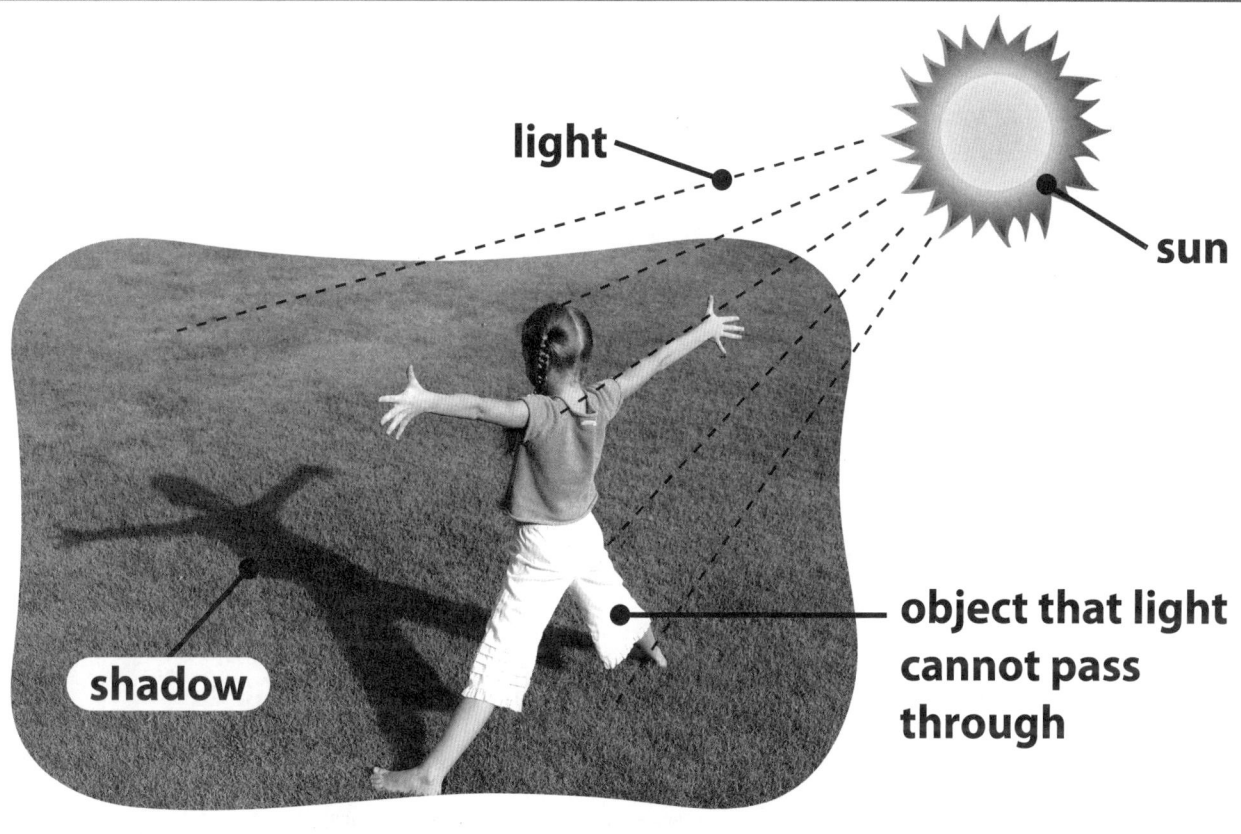

Earth Science 11

STEM Challenge: Making Shade

Challenge

Making Shade

Challenge: Build something that blocks light and makes shade for two small toys.

Testable goals: The shelter will block the sun and is 4 inches (10 centimeters) high and 4 inches (10 centimeters) wide.

Research: Think about things that give shade on a sunny day. Look at pictures of buildings, trees, and umbrellas. Notice the shapes of the objects and the materials they are made from.

Brainstorm: Think about all the different things that give shade. Think about what you will build to block light and make shade. Then draw a picture of it in the box.

STEM Challenge: Making Shade

Suggested Materials List

Items for each group

- ☐ glue
- ☐ tape
- ☐ string
- ☐ scissors

Items for the whole class

- ☐ cardboard
- ☐ paper
- ☐ plastic wrap
- ☐ wax paper
- ☐ craft sticks
- ☐ paper towel rolls
- ☐ straws
- ☐ _____
- ☐ _____
- ☐ _____
- ☐ _____
- ☐ _____
- ☐ _____
- ☐ _____

Items for testing

- ☐ ruler
- ☐ two small toys
- ☐ sunlight or flashlight

STEM Challenge: Making Shade

Think About the Design Process

Plan
Think about the things you have. How can you use them to build something that blocks light and gives shade to small toys?

Create
Look at the design you drew. Then use the things you have to build something that blocks light.

Test
Place two small toys under what you built. Does it stay up? Does light shine through it? Is it 4 inches high and 4 inches wide?

How Did It Work?
Think about what happened during your tests. Did your design work? What can you do to make it better?

Plan, create, and test until you are happy with what you built.

STEM Challenge: Making Shade

Design Process

 **Plan:** Write about your design. Tell what things you will use. Then draw your design.

 **Create**

 **Test:** Write about or draw to show what happened when you did your tests.

 **How Did It Work?** Write what you think.

Earth Science

STEM Challenge: Making Shade

Redesign Process

 **Redesign:** Write about what you will change. Draw your new design.

 **Change It or Make It Again**

 **Test:** Write about or draw to show what happened when you did your tests.

 **How Did It Work?** Write what you think.

Earth Science

STEM Challenge: Natural Homes

Task: Students will work in small groups to design a house for two small toys using only natural resources.

Getting Started

Build Content Knowledge
If you wish to provide students with background knowledge about natural resources, reproduce and distribute pages 18 and 19. Preview the Visual Literacy page with students. Then read the Science Concept page to students as they follow along, or, if they are able, have them read it independently. Next, discuss the science concept and the visual literacy graphics on those pages.

Introduce the Challenge
Reproduce and distribute the STEM Challenge on page 20. Then have students read the challenge and the testable goals. Discuss the materials with the students and decide on a plan for gathering the materials.

Next help students research natural resources in their neighborhood. Ask them to think about how science, technology, engineering, and math can be used to create a home using only natural resources. Finally, have students independently brainstorm and draw their ideas on page 20.

Completing the Challenge

Assign students to small groups.

Optional: Model the Design Process
You may wish to reproduce and distribute page 22 to students. This resource is intended to help students think about how to approach each step in the design process.

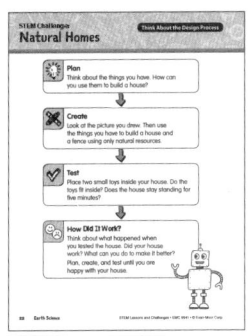

Design Process Worksheets
Reproduce and distribute the STEM design process worksheets to students. Provide support when needed to help students describe and evaluate their plans.

After the Challenge
Have students share their design processes, compare their homes, and brainstorm ideas for improvements.

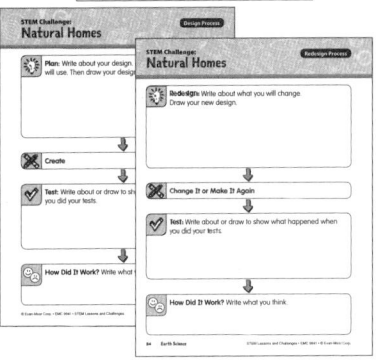

STEM Challenge: Natural Homes

Science Concept

Natural Resources

Our world is made up of natural resources. **Natural resources** are things that come from nature. They are not made by people. Water, plants, animals, and soil are all natural resources.

Different places in the world each have their own natural resources. Seashells, sand, and sea gulls are natural resources found along the shoreline of California. In the savannah of Kenya, some natural resources are mud, grass, and lions.

A group of people called the Maasai use only natural resources to build their homes. The Maasai live in Kenya and Tanzania. These countries are in East Africa. The Maasai build huts where they eat, sleep, and cook. The huts are made from mud, grass, tree branches, and cow dung. A fence made from wood and thorn bushes helps protect the huts. The thorns act like sharp needles. The fences keep out strangers and wild animals such as lions and hyenas. Without natural resources, people on Earth would not be able to survive.

STEM Challenge: Natural Homes

Visual Literacy

Natural resources are things that come from nature.

water

plants

animals

soil

Maasai huts are made from natural resources.

Maasai huts are protected by thorn fences.

fence

STEM Challenge: Natural Homes

Challenge

Natural Homes

Challenge: Build a house that will fit two small toys and has a fence around it.

Testable goals: The house fits two small toys, stands on its own for five minutes, and has a fence to protect it.

Research: Look at pictures of Maasai huts and fences. Notice the things used to make them. Find out where the Maasai live and the natural resources that are in that area. Look at the natural resources around your neighborhood.

Brainstorm: Think about all the different ways a house can look. Think about the house you want to build. Then draw a picture of it in the box.

STEM Challenge: Natural Homes

Suggested Materials List

Item for each group

- ☐ newspapers or plastic tubs to keep desks clean while working

Items for the whole class

- ☐ clay
- ☐ sand
- ☐ water
- ☐ twigs or sticks
- ☐ rocks
- ☐ leaves
- ☐ grass
- ☐ feathers

- ☐ _____
- ☐ _____
- ☐ _____
- ☐ _____
- ☐ _____
- ☐ _____
- ☐ _____
- ☐ _____

Items for testing

- ☐ two small toys
- ☐ clock or stopwatch

STEM Challenge: Natural Homes

Think About the Design Process

Plan
Think about the things you have. How can you use them to build a house?

Create
Look at the picture you drew. Then use the things you have to build a house and a fence using only natural resources.

Test
Place two small toys inside your house. Do the toys fit inside? Does the house stay standing for five minutes?

How Did It Work?
Think about what happened when you tested the house. Did your house work? What can you do to make it better?

Plan, create, and test until you are happy with your house.

STEM Challenge: Natural Homes

Design Process

Plan: Write about your design. Tell what things you will use. Then draw your design.

Create

Test: Write about or draw to show what happened when you did your tests.

How Did It Work? Write what you think.

STEM Challenge: Natural Homes

Redesign Process

 **Redesign:** Write about what you will change. Draw your new design.

 **Change It or Make It Again**

 **Test:** Write about or draw to show what happened when you did your tests.

 **How Did It Work?** Write what you think.

STEM Challenge: Tower

Task: Students will work in small groups to design a tall tower that can stand up on its own.

Getting Started

Build Content Knowledge
If you wish to provide students with background knowledge about gravity and how buildings stay standing, reproduce and distribute pages 26 and 27. Preview the Visual Literacy page with students. Then read the Science Concept page to students as they follow along, or, if they are able, have them read it independently. Next, discuss the science concept and the visual literacy graphics on those pages.

Introduce the Challenge
Reproduce and distribute the STEM Challenge on page 28. Then have students read the challenge and the testable goals. Discuss the materials with the students and decide on a plan for gathering the materials.

Next help students research tall buildings. Ask them to think about how science, technology, engineering, and math can be used to create a tall tower. Finally, have students independently brainstorm and draw their ideas on page 28.

Completing the Challenge

Assign students to small groups.

Optional: Model the Design Process
You may wish to reproduce and distribute page 30 to students. This resource is intended to help students think about how to approach each step in the design process.

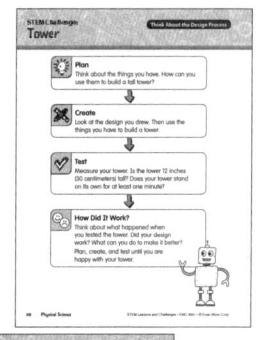

Design Process Worksheets
Reproduce and distribute the STEM design process worksheets to students. Provide support when needed to help students describe and evaluate their plans.

After the Challenge
Have students share their design processes, compare their towers, and brainstorm ideas for improvements.

© Evan-Moor Corp. • EMC 9941 • STEM Lessons and Challenges

Physical Science 25

STEM Challenge: Tower

Science Concept

Standing Tall

The Burj Khalifa is the tallest building in the world. It stands 828 meters, or 2,716 feet, high. That is as tall as 9 Statues of Liberty stacked on top of each other! But how does such a tall building stay standing? There are two things a tall building needs to stay up. It needs a strong base, and it needs to be balanced.

Gravity is a force that pulls things down to the ground. A tall building must have a strong **base**, or bottom, to keep gravity from pulling the top of the building down. Think about when you build with blocks. The biggest blocks have to be on the bottom, and the smaller blocks have to be on top, or the tower will tip over.

A building must also be **balanced**. Things are balanced when there is an equal amount of weight on each side. For example, a boy walks on a thin beam. He needs to stay balanced to stay on the beam. If he moves too much to one side, he will fall. The wind is a force that can push a building off balance and tip it over.

STEM Challenge: Tower

Visual Literacy

The Burj Khalifa

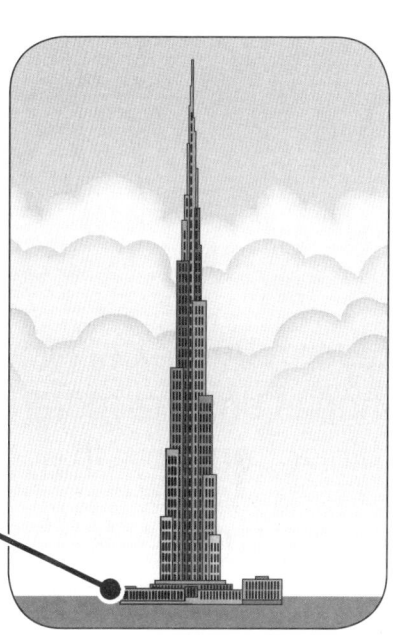

The strong, wide base of the Burj Khalifa keeps the tall building from falling.

Balanced

Off Balance or Not Balanced

STEM Challenge: Tower

Tower

Challenge: Make a tall tower that can stand on its own.

Testable goals: The tower will stand 12 inches (30 centimeters) high. It will stand on its own for one minute.

Research: Look at pictures of tall buildings and towers. Notice their shapes and the materials the buildings and towers are made from. Think about how they stand up to the forces of gravity and wind.

Brainstorm: Think about all the different ways a tower can look. Think about the tower you want to build. Then draw a picture of it in the box.

STEM Challenge: Tower

Suggested Materials List

Item for each group

- ☐ tape

Items for the whole class

- ☐ index cards
- ☐ lined notebook paper
- ☐ tissue paper
- ☐ wax paper

- ☐ _____
- ☐ _____
- ☐ _____
- ☐ _____

Items for testing

- ☐ ruler or tape measure
- ☐ stopwatch or clock

STEM Challenge: Tower

Think About the Design Process

Plan
Think about the things you have. How can you use them to build a tall tower?

Create
Look at the design you drew. Then use the things you have to build a tower.

Test
Measure your tower. Is the tower 12 inches (30 centimeters) tall? Does your tower stand on its own for at least one minute?

How Did It Work?
Think about what happened when you tested the tower. Did your design work? What can you do to make it better?

Plan, create, and test until you are happy with your tower.

STEM Challenge: Tower

Design Process

Plan: Write about your design. Tell what things you will use. Then draw your design.

Create

Test: Write about or draw to show what happened when you did your tests.

How Did It Work? Write what you think.

© Evan-Moor Corp. • EMC 9941 • STEM Lessons and Challenges   Physical Science   31

STEM Challenge: Tower

Redesign Process

Redesign: Write about what you will change. Draw your new design.

Change It or Make It Again

Test: Write about or draw to show what happened when you did your tests.

How Did It Work? Write what you think.

STEM Challenge: Maraca Music

Task: Students will work in small groups to design two maracas that make two different sounds.

Getting Started

Build Content Knowledge
If you wish to provide students with background knowledge about sound waves and vibrations, reproduce and distribute pages 34 and 35. Preview the Visual Literacy page with students. Then read the Science Concept page to students as they follow along, or, if they are able, have them read it independently. Next, discuss the science concept and the visual literacy graphics on those pages.

Introduce the Challenge
Reproduce and distribute the STEM Challenge on page 36. Then have students read the challenge and the testable goal. Discuss the materials with the students and decide on a plan for gathering the materials.

Next help students research ways to make different sounds. Ask them to think about how science, technology, engineering, and math can be used to create maracas that make different sounds. Finally, have students independently brainstorm and draw their ideas on page 36.

Completing the Challenge

Assign students to small groups.

Optional: Model the Design Process
You may wish to reproduce and distribute page 38 to students. This resource is intended to help students think about how to approach each step in the design process.

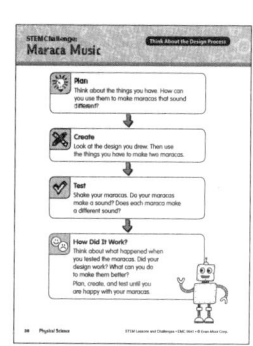

Design Process Worksheets
Reproduce and distribute the STEM design process worksheets to students. Provide support when needed to help students describe and evaluate their plans.

After the Challenge
Have students share their design processes, compare their maracas, and brainstorm ideas for improvements.

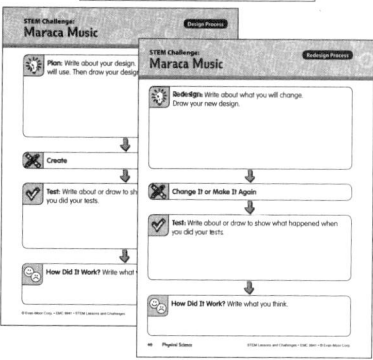

STEM Challenge: Maraca Music

Science Concept

Vibrations and Music

Sounds are all around us. A bird chirps, a bell rings, and a drum goes *boom!* But how are sounds made? Sound comes from vibrations. When something **vibrates**, or shakes, it moves back and forth. The vibrations make **sound waves**. The sound waves move through the air and into your ear.

Some sound waves are musical. You can hear them when an instrument is played. When you hit a drum or pluck a guitar string, it vibrates. A **maraca** is an instrument that makes a sound when you shake it. Some maracas are made from a large round fruit called a gourd. The fruit has a hard shell. The hard shell is filled with seeds or pebbles. When you shake the maraca, the seeds or pebbles hit the hard shell. Sound waves move through the air, and people hear the sound of the maracas.

Not all maracas sound the same. A maraca filled with seeds sounds different from a maraca filled with pebbles. Shaking the maraca hard can make a loud sound. Shaking a maraca softly makes a softer sound.

STEM Challenge: Maraca Music

Visual Literacy

Hitting a drum makes vibrations.

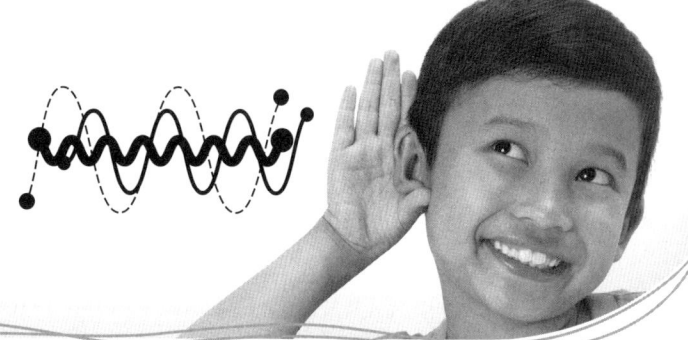

Vibrations make sound waves. You can hear sound waves, but you cannot see them.

Maracas made from a gourd

Hard outside

Handle for easy shaking

Seeds inside

Physical Science

STEM Challenge: Maraca Music

Maraca Music

Challenge: Make two maracas that have different sounds.

Testable goal: When you shake the maracas, you can hear two different sounds.

Research: Look at pictures of maracas. Notice the shape of the maracas and the materials they are made from. Think about how the things inside maracas make a certain sound.

Brainstorm: Think about how different maracas have different sounds. Think about the sounds you want your maracas to have. Then draw a picture of the maracas you will make and what you will put in them.

Physical Science

STEM Challenge: Maraca Music

Suggested Materials List

Items for each group

- [ ] glue
- [ ] tape
- [ ] scissors

Items for the whole class

- [ ] beans (uncooked)
- [ ] beads
- [ ] cotton balls
- [ ] seeds (corn, sunflower, etc.)
- [ ] rice (uncooked)
- [ ] paper
- [ ] paper towel rolls
- [ ] plastic cups
- [ ] plastic eggs
- [ ] craft sticks
- [ ] spoons
- [ ] yogurt cups (emptied and cleaned)
- [ ] _____
- [ ] _____
- [ ] _____
- [ ] _____
- [ ] _____
- [ ] _____

STEM Challenge: Maraca Music

Think About the Design Process

Plan
Think about the things you have. How can you use them to make maracas that sound different?

Create
Look at the design you drew. Then use the things you have to make two maracas.

Test
Shake your maracas. Do your maracas make a sound? Does each maraca make a different sound?

How Did It Work?
Think about what happened when you tested the maracas. Did your design work? What can you do to make them better?

Plan, create, and test until you are happy with your maracas.

STEM Challenge: Maraca Music

Design Process

 **Plan:** Write about your design. Tell what things you will use. Then draw your design.

 **Create**

 **Test:** Write about or draw to show what happened when you did your tests.

 **How Did It Work?** Write what you think.

STEM Challenge: Maraca Music

Redesign Process

 **Redesign:** Write about what you will change. Draw your new design.

 **Change It or Make It Again**

 **Test:** Write about or draw to show what happened when you did your tests.

 **How Did It Work?** Write what you think.

STEM Challenge: Strong Roofs

Task: Students will work in small groups to build a roof for a house model that can withstand the weight of a heavy snow substitute.

Getting Started

Build Content Knowledge
If you wish to provide students with background knowledge about force and weight, reproduce and distribute pages 42 and 43. Preview the Visual Literacy page with students. Then read the Science Concept page to students as they follow along, or, if they are able, have them read it independently. Next, discuss the science concept and the visual literacy graphics on those pages.

Introduce the Challenge
Reproduce and distribute the STEM Challenge on page 44. Then have students read the challenge and the testable goals. Discuss the materials with the students and decide on a plan for gathering the materials.

Next help students research the shapes of roofs. Ask them to think about how science, technology, engineering, and math can be used to create a roof. Finally, have students independently brainstorm and draw their ideas on page 44.

Completing the Challenge

Assign students to small groups.

Optional: Model the Design Process
You may wish to reproduce and distribute page 46 to students. This resource is intended to help students think about how to approach each step in the design process.

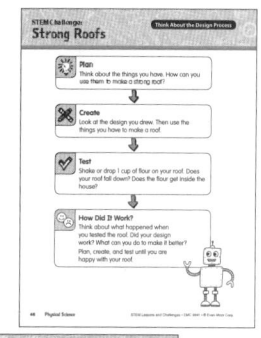

Design Process Worksheets
Reproduce and distribute the STEM design process worksheets to students. Provide support when needed to help students describe and evaluate their plans.

After the Challenge
Have students share their design processes, compare their roofs, and brainstorm ideas for improvements.

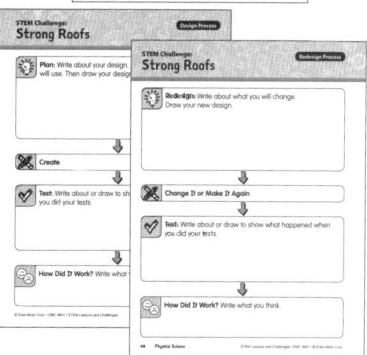

STEM Challenge: Strong Roofs

Science Concept

Forces on the Roof

In some places around the world, it snows. Architects and engineers, people who plan and build houses, think about how much snow piles on the roof when they build new homes. A **roof** is the top of a building. It protects people and animals from the weather outside. It is important to make a roof strong and the right shape. If a roof is strong, it will keep out the snow, wind, and rain. If a roof is not strong, it will **cave in**, or break, when a strong force such as a falling tree hits it.

A **force** is a push or pull. Forces can make things move, stay in place, go faster or slower, or change direction. Forces push and pull on things like a tug-of-war. The strongest force makes the biggest change. We may not see them, but forces push and pull buildings all the time. When the wind blows, the force of the wind pushes against a building. When snow falls and piles on a roof, it pushes down on the roof. How heavy something is or how much force an object has is called a **load**. The bigger the load, the more force it has. The more force it has, the more change it can make.

STEM Challenge: Strong Roofs

Visual Literacy

Force of the snow

The heavy snow made the roof fall in.

Force of the roof

Types of Roofs

Gable roof

Flat roof

Curved roof

Physical Science

STEM Challenge: Strong Roofs

Strong Roofs

Challenge: Make a strong roof that can hold a load of flour.

Testable goals: The roof will cover a house model and will not fall down when 1 cup of flour is poured on it.

Research: Look at pictures of different roofs. Notice the shape of the roofs. Think about what makes a roof strong and what happens when snow piles up on a roof.

Brainstorm: Think about all the different ways a roof can look. Think about the roof you want to build. Then draw a picture of it in the box.

STEM Challenge: Strong Roofs

Suggested Materials List

Items for each group

- ☐ glue
- ☐ tape
- ☐ scissors

- ☐ **house model:** Provide each group with a shoe box (with no lid) to act as the house model.

Items for the whole class

- ☐ aluminum foil
- ☐ paper
- ☐ tissue paper
- ☐ index cards
- ☐ craft sticks
- ☐ pipe cleaners

- ☐ straws
- ☐ _____
- ☐ _____
- ☐ _____
- ☐ _____

Items for testing

- ☐ flour
- ☐ flour sifter (optional)
- ☐ 1-cup measuring cup
- ☐ house model

STEM Challenge: Strong Roofs

Think About the Design Process

Plan
Think about the things you have. How can you use them to make a strong roof?

Create
Look at the design you drew. Then use the things you have to make a roof.

Test
Shake or drop 1 cup of flour on your roof. Does your roof fall down? Does the flour get inside the house?

How Did It Work?
Think about what happened when you tested the roof. Did your design work? What can you do to make it better?

Plan, create, and test until you are happy with your roof.

STEM Challenge: Strong Roofs

Design Process

 **Plan:** Write about your design. Tell what things you will use. Then draw your design.

 **Create**

 **Test:** Write about or draw to show what happened when you did your tests.

 **How Did It Work?** Write what you think.

© Evan-Moor Corp. • EMC 9941 • STEM Lessons and Challenges   **Physical Science**   47

STEM Challenge: Strong Roofs

Redesign Process

Redesign: Write about what you will change. Draw your new design.

Change It or Make It Again

Test: Write about or draw to show what happened when you did your tests.

How Did It Work? Write what you think.

STEM Challenge: Telephone

Task: Students will work in small groups to design a device that will allow them to hear and talk to someone from a distance of 10 feet (3 meters).

Getting Started

Build Content Knowledge
If you wish to provide students with background knowledge about sound waves, reproduce and distribute pages 50 and 51. Preview the Visual Literacy page with students. Then read the Science Concept page to students as they follow along, or, if they are able, have them read it independently. Next, discuss the science concept and the visual literacy graphics on those pages.

Introduce the Challenge
Reproduce and distribute the STEM Challenge on page 52. Then have students read the challenge and the testable goal. Discuss the materials with the students and decide on a plan for gathering the materials.

Next help students research telephones and materials that sound can travel through. Ask them to think about how science, technology, engineering, and math can be used to create a telephone. Finally, have students independently brainstorm and draw their ideas on page 52.

Completing the Challenge

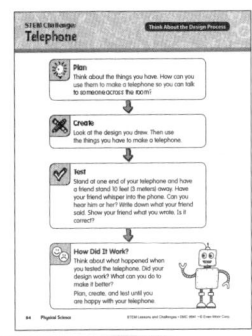

Assign students to small groups.

Optional: Model the Design Process
You may wish to reproduce and distribute page 54 to students. This resource is intended to help students think about how to approach each step in the design process.

Design Process Worksheets
Reproduce and distribute the STEM design process worksheets to students. Provide support when needed to help students describe and evaluate their plans.

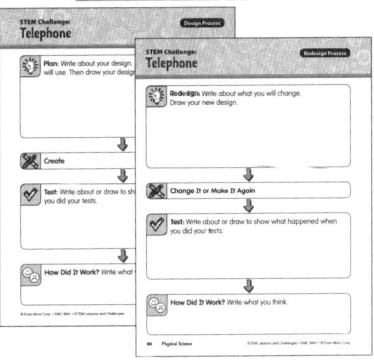

After the Challenge
Have students share their design processes, compare their telephones, and brainstorm ideas for improvements.

Physical Science 49

STEM Challenge: Telephone

Science Concept

Sound Waves

Have you ever thrown a rock into a lake? When the rock hits the water, the water makes ripples, or waves, in all directions. Sound moves in the same way. Sounds are made when objects **vibrate**, or shake back and forth very fast. The vibration then makes **sound waves** that move like ripples or waves in water.

Sound waves can move through air, liquid, and solids. Sound waves move the fastest through solids. A table and a guitar string are solids. Try putting your ear on a table and tapping the table with your finger. You can hear the tapping because the sound waves traveled through the table and into your ear. Sound waves also move through the strings of a guitar when you pluck or pull on the strings.

Our ears help us hear. The **pinna** is the part of the ear that we can see. The shape of the pinna helps sound waves move through a short tube called the **ear canal**. The **eardrum** is at the end of the ear canal. Sound waves hit the skin of the eardrum and make it vibrate. Then our brain tells us what we are hearing.

STEM Challenge: Telephone

Visual Literacy

Sound waves move through the air when we talk.

Sound waves move through a solid like a guitar string.

Whales use sounds under the water to tell each other things.

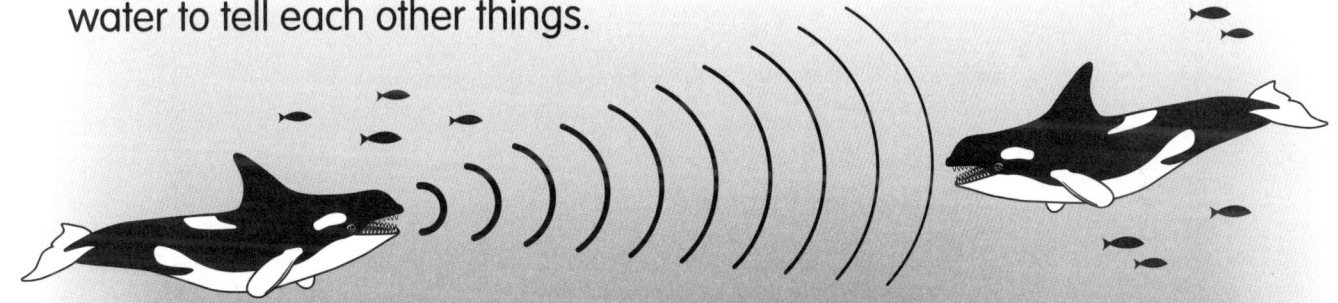

Sound moves through the ear and vibrates the eardrum.

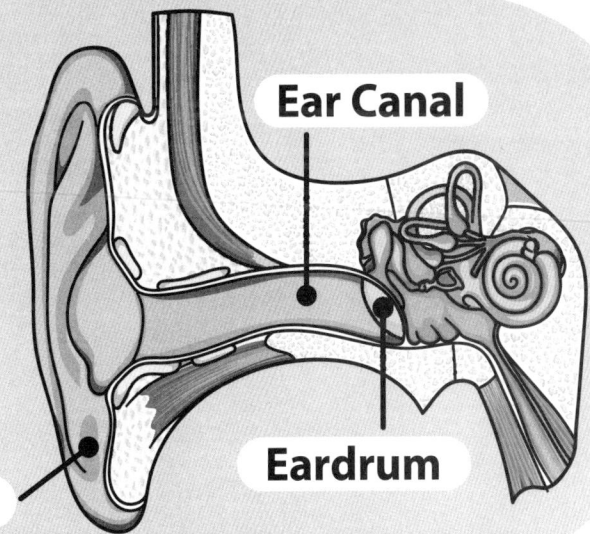

Ear Canal

Sound

Pinna

Eardrum

Physical Science

STEM Challenge:
Telephone

Challenge

Telephone

Challenge: Make a telephone that will allow you to hear and talk to someone 10 feet (3 meters) away.

Testable goal: Listen through the telephone to someone whispering a sentence. Write what you hear.

Research: Look at pictures of old telephones. Notice the shape of the phones. Think about how sound waves move and what things they can move through.

Brainstorm: Think about the different ways a telephone can look. Think about the telephone you want to build. Then draw a picture of it in the box.

52 Physical Science STEM Lessons and Challenges • EMC 9941 • © Evan-Moor Corp.

STEM Challenge: Telephone

Suggested Materials List

Items for each group

- [ ] glue
- [ ] tape
- [ ] scissors

Items for the whole class

- [ ] string
- [ ] fishing wire
- [ ] yarn
- [ ] pool noodle
- [ ] paper towel rolls
- [ ] straws
- [ ] paper cups
- [ ] funnels
- [ ] paper clips
- [ ] washers
- [ ] _____
- [ ] _____
- [ ] _____
- [ ] _____

Items for testing

- [ ] pencil
- [ ] paper
- [ ] ruler or tape measure

STEM Challenge: Telephone

Think About the Design Process

 **Plan**
Think about the things you have. How can you use them to make a telephone so you can talk to someone across the room?

 **Create**
Look at the design you drew. Then use the things you have to make a telephone.

 **Test**
Stand at one end of your telephone and have a friend stand 10 feet (3 meters) away. Have your friend whisper into the phone. Can you hear him or her? Write down what your friend said. Show your friend what you wrote. Is it correct?

 **How Did It Work?**
Think about what happened when you tested the telephone. Did your design work? What can you do to make it better?

Plan, create, and test until you are happy with your telephone.

STEM Challenge: Telephone

Design Process

 **Plan:** Write about your design. Tell what things you will use. Then draw your design.

 **Create**

 **Test:** Write about or draw to show what happened when you did your tests.

 **How Did It Work?** Write what you think.

STEM Challenge: Telephone

Redesign Process

 **Redesign:** Write about what you will change. Draw your new design.

 **Change It or Make It Again**

 **Test:** Write about or draw to show what happened when you did your tests.

 **How Did It Work?** Write what you think.

STEM Challenge: Soft Landing

Task: Students will work in small groups to design a cup that lands gently enough that a ball inside doesn't bounce out.

Getting Started

Build Content Knowledge

If you wish to provide students with background knowledge about gravity and how shock absorbers help with soft landings, reproduce and distribute pages 58 and 59. Preview the Visual Literacy page with students. Then read the Science Concept page to students as they follow along, or, if they are able, have them read it independently. Next, discuss the science concept and the visual literacy graphics on those pages.

Introduce the Challenge

Reproduce and distribute the STEM Challenge on page 60. Then have students read the challenge and the testable goals. Discuss the materials with the students and decide on a plan for gathering the materials.

Next help students research objects that have shock absorbers. Ask them to think about how science, technology, engineering, and math can be used to create a device that helps a cup holding a ball land safely. Finally, have students independently brainstorm and draw their ideas on page 60.

Completing the Challenge

Assign students to small groups.

Optional: Model the Design Process

You may wish to reproduce and distribute page 62 to students. This resource is intended to help students think about how to approach each step in the design process.

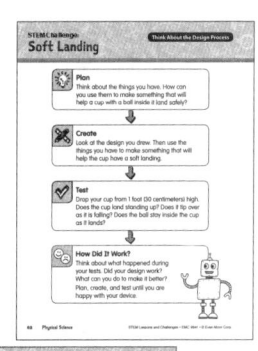

Design Process Worksheets

Reproduce and distribute the STEM design process worksheets to students. Provide support when needed to help students describe and evaluate their plans.

After the Challenge

Have students share their design processes, compare their cups, and brainstorm ideas for improvements.

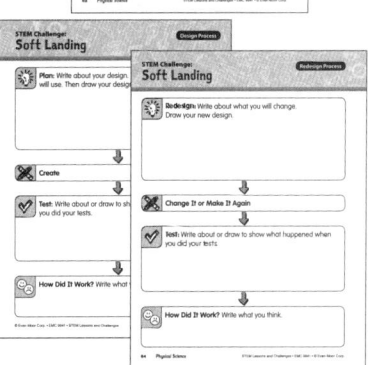

STEM Challenge: Soft Landing

Science Concept

Taking in Energy

When you throw a ball up in the air, the ball falls back down to the ground. Why does this happen? It happens because of a force called **gravity**. Gravity is a force that pulls things together. People would float up in space if there was no gravity. The force of gravity on Earth pulls everything down to the ground.

An object like a ball uses energy as it falls down. An object that falls fast has more energy than an object that falls slowly. The more energy the object has, the harder it will hit the floor. An object needs a **shock absorber** to help it have a soft landing. A **shock** is a hit or force. When an object **absorbs**, it takes in or sucks up something like a sponge absorbs water. A shock absorber helps an object land more softly by sucking up the energy from a hit or force.

Springs and squishy things are used as shock absorbers in airplanes, beds, and shoes. Falling on hard ground can hurt you. Falling on a bed that is filled with springs and squishy things will not. Our bodies have shock absorbers, too. When we jump up high, our knees bend when we land. They absorb energy like a spring.

STEM Challenge: Soft Landing

Visual Literacy

An apple falls down to the ground because of the force of gravity.

Thick rubber on the bottom of shoes helps take in the energy from the crash of your feet hitting the ground.

Inside of the bed

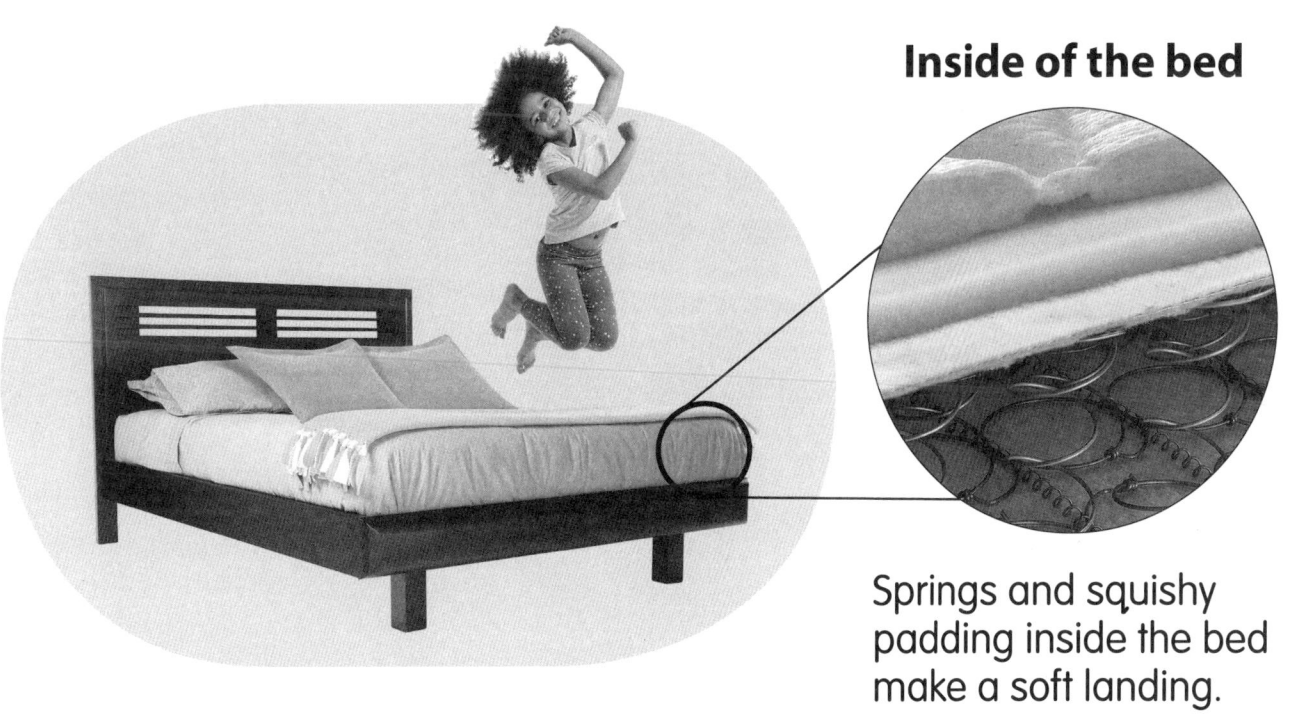

Springs and squishy padding inside the bed make a soft landing.

STEM Challenge: Soft Landing

Soft Landing

Challenge: Make a cup with a ball in it land safely.

Testable goals: When you drop the cup from 1 foot (30 centimeters) high, it will land standing up. The ball will still be in the cup. The cup will not be covered. The ball will be able to move inside the cup.

Research: Look at pictures of things that have shock absorbers to soften a landing. Notice the shape they have. Think about what materials they are made from.

Brainstorm: Think about all the different things that have shock absorbers to soften a landing. Think about the cup you want to make. Then draw a picture of it in the box.

STEM Challenge: Soft Landing

Suggested Materials List

Items for each group

- ☐ glue
- ☐ tape
- ☐ paper cup
- ☐ table tennis ball

Items for the whole class

- ☐ paper
- ☐ tissue paper
- ☐ index cards
- ☐ straws
- ☐ cotton balls
- ☐ marshmallows
- ☐ fasteners
- ☐ string
- ☐ cardboard
- ☐ _____
- ☐ _____
- ☐ _____
- ☐ _____

Items for testing

- ☐ ruler or measuring tape
- ☐ table tennis ball

STEM Challenge: Soft Landing

Think About the Design Process

Plan
Think about the things you have. How can you use them to make something that will help a cup with a ball inside it land safely?

Create
Look at the design you drew. Then use the things you have to make something that will help the cup have a soft landing.

Test
Drop your cup from 1 foot (30 centimeters) high. Does the cup land standing up? Does it tip over as it is falling? Does the ball stay inside the cup as it lands?

How Did It Work?
Think about what happened during your tests. Did your design work? What can you do to make it better?

Plan, create, and test until you are happy with your device.

STEM Challenge: Soft Landing

Design Process

Plan: Write about your design. Tell what things you will use. Then draw your design.

 **Create**

 **Test:** Write about or draw to show what happened when you did your tests.

 **How Did It Work?** Write what you think.

STEM Challenge: Soft Landing

Redesign Process

Redesign: Write about what you will change. Draw your new design.

Change It or Make It Again

Test: Write about or draw to show what happened when you did your tests.

How Did It Work? Write what you think.

STEM Challenge: Bridge

Task: Students will work in small groups to design a bridge that can hold weight.

Getting Started

Build Content Knowledge
If you wish to provide students with background knowledge about types of bridges, reproduce and distribute pages 66 and 67. Preview the Visual Literacy page with students. Then read the Science Concept page to students as they follow along, or, if they are able, have them read it independently. Next, discuss the science concept and the visual literacy graphics on those pages.

Introduce the Challenge
Reproduce and distribute the STEM Challenge on page 68. Then have students read the challenge and the testable goals. Discuss the materials with the students and decide on a plan for gathering the materials.

Next help students research different types of bridges. Ask them to think about how science, technology, engineering, and math can be used to create a strong bridge. Finally, have students independently brainstorm and draw their ideas on page 68.

Completing the Challenge

Assign students to small groups.

Optional: Model the Design Process
You may wish to reproduce and distribute page 70 to students. This resource is intended to help students think about how to approach each step in the design process.

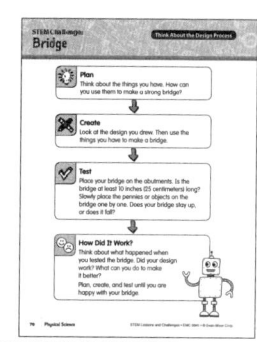

Design Process Worksheets
Reproduce and distribute the STEM design process worksheets to students. Provide support when needed to help students describe and evaluate their plans.

After the Challenge
Have students share their design processes, compare their bridges, and brainstorm ideas for improvements.

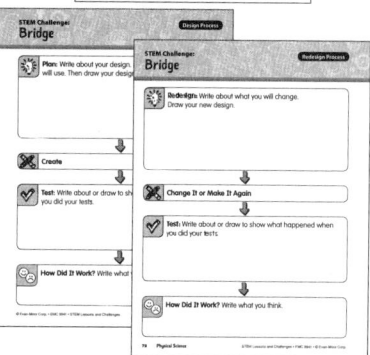

Physical Science

STEM Challenge: Bridge

Science Concept

Forces on Shapes

People use bridges to help them travel over rivers or valleys. **Engineers** are people who plan and make the bridges. Engineers must think about the forces that push and pull on a bridge. They must make sure it is strong and safe. A **force** is a push or pull. Weight is one thing that pushes down on a bridge. Engineers build bridges in different shapes so they can hold a lot of weight without falling or breaking. Here are three types of bridges. Each has a different shape.

A **beam bridge** has one long beam held up by abutments at each end. **Abutments** are the strong parts that all bridges rest on. They keep the bridge standing. Heavy weight or a large force on a beam bridge can make it fall or break in the middle.

An **arch bridge** has an arch, or half circle, under a beam. The shape of the arch helps the top of the bridge hold a lot of weight.

Lastly, a **truss bridge** is made up of triangles. Triangles are a strong shape because they do not bend easily when a force pushes or pulls on them. That is why truss bridges can hold a lot of weight.

STEM Challenge: Bridge

Visual Literacy

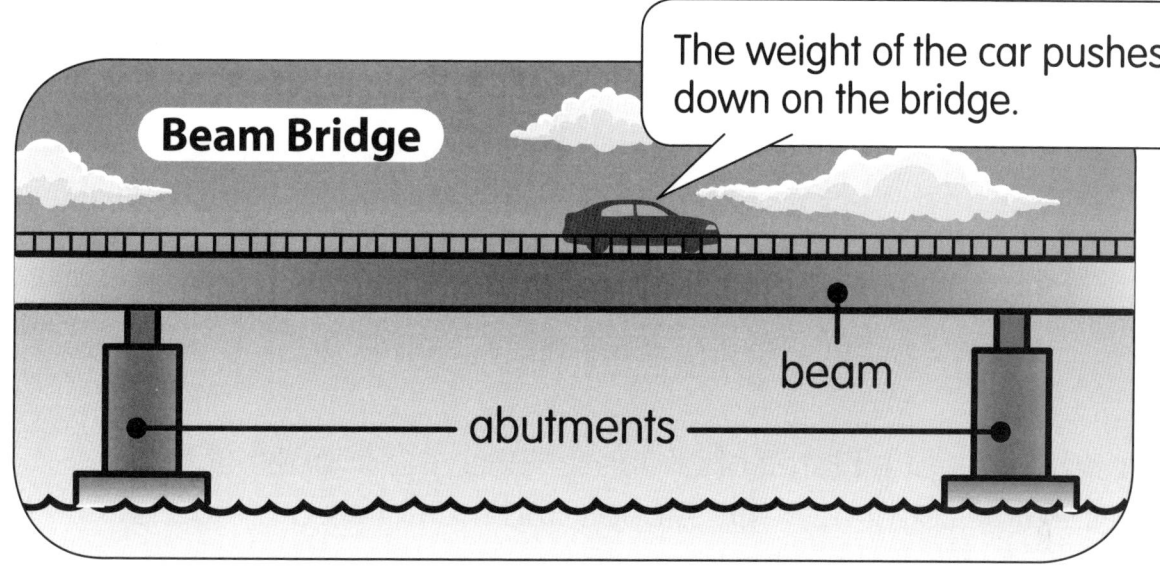

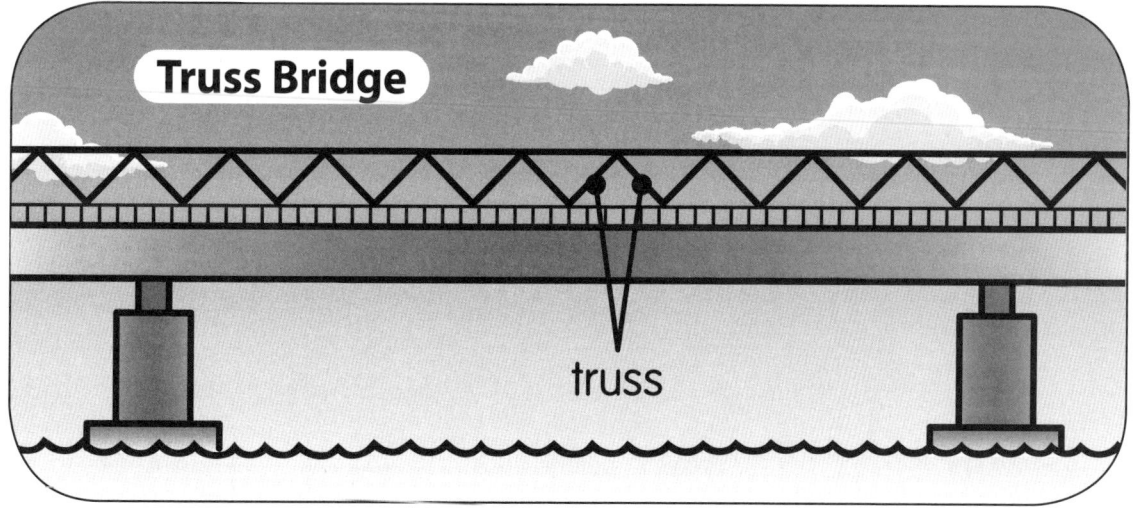

STEM Challenge: Bridge

Challenge

Bridge

Challenge: Make a bridge that can hold a small amount of weight.

Testable goals: The bridge will be 10 inches (25 centimeters) long. The bridge will hold 22 pennies or 2 ounces without falling or breaking.

Research: Look at pictures of bridges. Notice the shapes of the bridges. Think about how the shapes and the things a bridge is made out of can make a bridge strong or weak.

Brainstorm: Think about the three different types of bridges. Think about the bridge you want to build. Then draw a picture of it in the box.

STEM Challenge: Bridge

Suggested Materials List

Items for each group

- ☐ tape
- ☐ scissors
- ☐ **abutments:** Provide each group with abutments made from blocks or paper towel rolls to place bridges on.

Items for the whole class

- ☐ toothpicks
- ☐ uncooked spaghetti
- ☐ craft sticks
- ☐ straws
- ☐ paper
- ☐ gumdrops
- ☐ marshmallows
- ☐ _____
- ☐ _____
- ☐ _____

Items for testing

- ☐ ruler or tape measure
- ☐ 22 pennies or an object that weighs at least 2 ounces
- ☐ abutments

STEM Challenge: Bridge

Think About the Design Process

Plan
Think about the things you have. How can you use them to make a strong bridge?

Create
Look at the design you drew. Then use the things you have to make a bridge.

Test
Place your bridge on the abutments. Is the bridge at least 10 inches (25 centimeters) long? Slowly place the pennies or objects on the bridge one by one. Does your bridge stay up, or does it fall?

How Did It Work?
Think about what happened when you tested the bridge. Did your design work? What can you do to make it better?

Plan, create, and test until you are happy with your bridge.

STEM Challenge: Bridge

Design Process

 **Plan:** Write about your design. Tell what things you will use. Then draw your design.

 **Create**

 **Test:** Write about or draw to show what happened when you did your tests.

 **How Did It Work?** Write what you think.

STEM Challenge: Bridge

Redesign Process

Redesign: Write about what you will change. Draw your new design.

 **Change It or Make It Again**

 **Test:** Write about or draw to show what happened when you did your tests.

 **How Did It Work?** Write what you think.

STEM Challenge: Marble Roller Coaster

Task: Students will work in small groups to design a roller coaster for a marble.

Getting Started

Build Content Knowledge
If you wish to provide students with background knowledge about force, gravity, and motion, reproduce and distribute pages 74 and 75. Preview the Visual Literacy page with students. Then read the Science Concept page to students as they follow along, or, if they are able, have them read it independently. Next, discuss the science concept and the visual literacy graphics on those pages.

Introduce the Challenge
Reproduce and distribute the STEM Challenge on page 76. Then have students read the challenge and the testable goal. Discuss the materials with the students and decide on a plan for gathering the materials.

Next help students research different roller coasters. Ask them to think about how science, technology, engineering, and math can be used to create a roller coaster for a marble. Finally, have students independently brainstorm and draw their ideas on page 76.

Completing the Challenge

Assign students to small groups.

Optional: Model the Design Process
You may wish to reproduce and distribute page 78 to students. This resource is intended to help students think about how to approach each step in the design process.

Design Process Worksheets
Reproduce and distribute the STEM design process worksheets to students. Provide support when needed to help students describe and evaluate their plans.

After the Challenge
Have students share their design processes, compare their roller coasters, and brainstorm ideas for improvements.

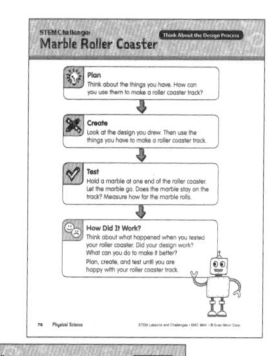

Physical Science 73

STEM Challenge: Marble Roller Coaster

Science Concept

How Roller Coasters Move

A roller coaster is a fun ride. A line of cars rolls on a track with hills. The first roller coasters were made out of wood. Wood tracks made the ride very bumpy. New roller coasters are made from a metal called steel. Steel is stronger than wood. It can bend to make better twists and turns. It can make higher hills. Steel is also smoother than wood. The car can travel faster on a smooth track.

A roller coaster does not have an engine that makes it move. Roller coasters use force to work. **Force** is a push or pull. A force can make objects speed up, slow down, and change direction. A force called **gravity** pulls all things down to the ground. Gravity is the force that helps a roller coaster move.

Most roller coasters start by moving up a big hill. At the top of the hill, gravity pulls the roller coaster car down the track. The car is now moving, or in **motion**. The car moves faster as it rolls down the hill. The higher the hill, the faster the car goes. This is because gravity has more time to pull the car down. The car needs a fast speed to move up and down more hills.

STEM Challenge: Marble Roller Coaster

Visual Literacy

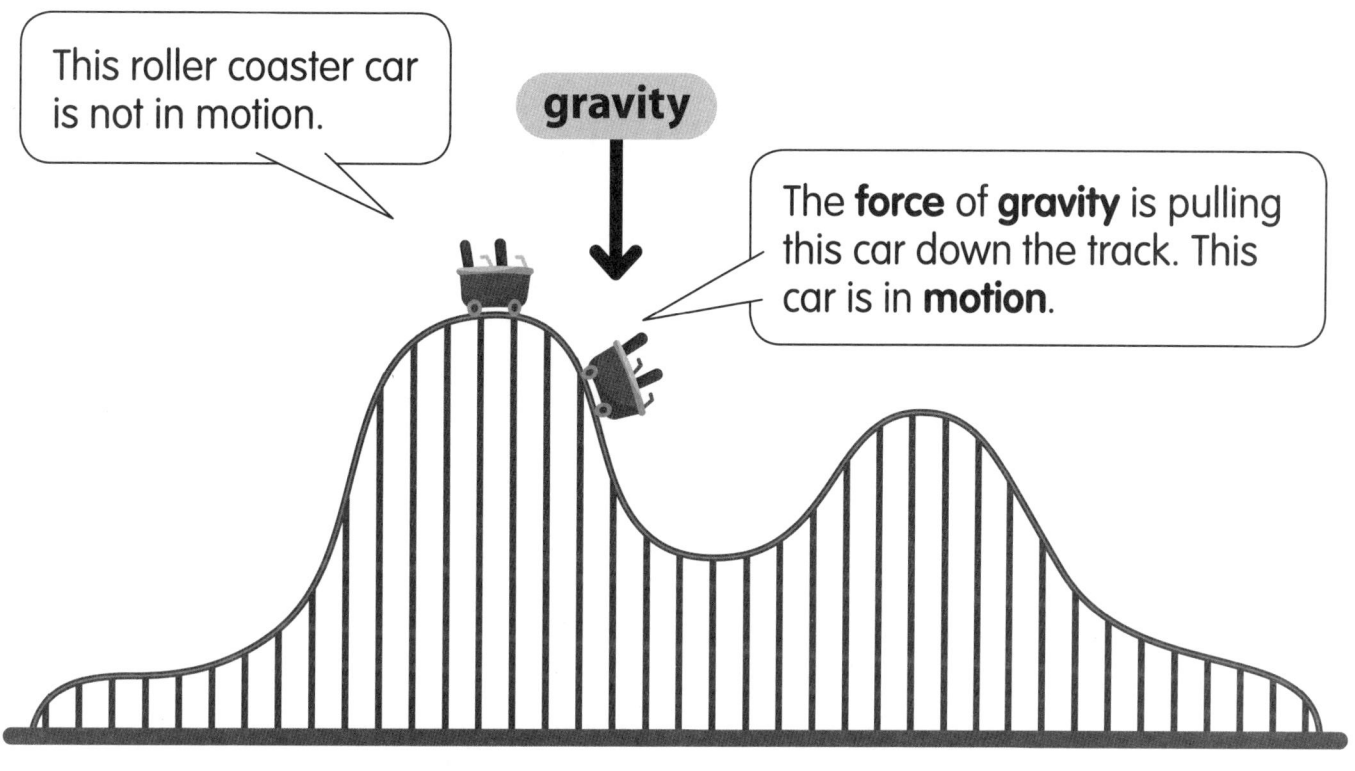

This roller coaster car is not in motion.

gravity

The **force** of **gravity** is pulling this car down the track. This car is in **motion**.

These cars can move up and down the second hill because they went down the first hill very fast.

Physical Science

STEM Challenge: Marble Roller Coaster

Challenge

Marble Roller Coaster

Challenge: Make a roller coaster track for a marble.

Testable goal: A marble will move 12 inches (30 centimeters) on the roller coaster track.

Research: Look at pictures of roller coasters. Notice what the roller coaster track is made out of. Think about the forces making a roller coaster car move.

Brainstorm: Think about all the different ways a roller coaster can look. Think about the roller coaster you want to build. Then draw a picture of it in the box.

STEM Challenge: Marble Roller Coaster

Suggested Materials List

Items for each group

- ☐ tape
- ☐ scissors
- ☐ marble

Items for the whole class

- ☐ paper towel rolls
- ☐ pool noodles
- ☐ foam pipe insulation
- ☐ cardboard
- ☐ construction paper
- ☐ sandpaper
- ☐ bubble wrap
- ☐ items to raise the coaster to make a hill (blocks, books, etc.)
- ☐ _____
- ☐ _____
- ☐ _____
- ☐ _____
- ☐ _____

Items for testing

- ☐ ruler
- ☐ marble

STEM Challenge: Marble Roller Coaster

Think About the Design Process

Plan
Think about the things you have. How can you use them to make a roller coaster track?

Create
Look at the design you drew. Then use the things you have to make a roller coaster track.

Test
Hold a marble at one end of the roller coaster. Let the marble go. Does the marble stay on the track? Measure how far the marble rolls.

How Did It Work?
Think about what happened when you tested your roller coaster. Did your design work? What can you do to make it better?

Plan, create, and test until you are happy with your roller coaster track.

STEM Challenge: Marble Roller Coaster

Design Process

 **Plan:** Write about your design. Tell what things you will use. Then draw your design.

 **Create**

 **Test:** Write about or draw to show what happened when you did your tests.

 **How Did It Work?** Write what you think.

STEM Challenge: Marble Roller Coaster

Redesign Process

 **Redesign:** Write about what you will change. Draw your new design.

 **Change It or Make It Again**

 **Test:** Write about or draw to show what happened when you did your tests.

 **How Did It Work?** Write what you think.

STEM Challenge: Sailboat

Task: Students will work in small groups to design a sail that uses the wind to move a boat at least 2 feet (60 centimeters).

Getting Started

Build Content Knowledge
If you wish to provide students with background knowledge about wind power and sails, reproduce and distribute pages 82 and 83. Preview the Visual Literacy page with students. Then read the Science Concept page to students as they follow along, or, if they are able, have them read it independently. Next, discuss the science concept and the visual literacy graphics on those pages.

Introduce the Challenge
Reproduce and distribute the STEM Challenge on page 84. Then have students read the challenge and the testable goals. Discuss the materials with the students and decide on a plan for gathering the materials.

Next help students research different shapes of sails. Ask them to think about how science, technology, engineering, and math can be used to create a sail that catches the wind to move a boat forward. Finally, have students independently brainstorm and draw their ideas on page 84.

Completing the Challenge

Assign students to small groups.

Optional: Model the Design Process
You may wish to reproduce and distribute page 86 to students. This resource is intended to help students think about how to approach each step in the design process.

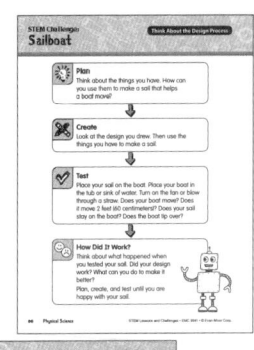

Design Process Worksheets
Reproduce and distribute the STEM design process worksheets to students. Provide support when needed to help students describe and evaluate their plans.

After the Challenge
Have students share their design processes, compare their sails, and brainstorm ideas for improvements.

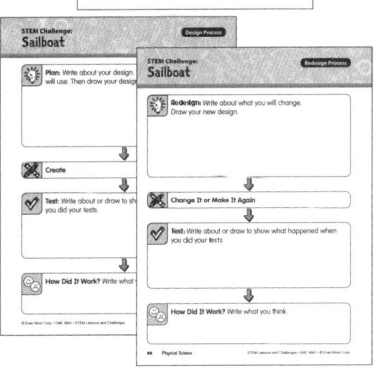

STEM Challenge: Sailboat

Science Concept

Catching the Wind

The **wind** is a powerful force. It can blow hard enough to push a person or a tree to the ground. It can even push a building down to the ground! The wind is also an important force that helps things live and grow. The wind cools people down on a hot, sunny day. The wind blows seeds around so that new plants grow in different places. The wind helps a flying squirrel glide from tree to tree. It also pushes sailboats across water.

A sailboat is a boat that uses wind to move. The **sail** on a boat is a large piece of cloth. The sail catches the wind and powers the boat. A long, strong pole called a **mast** helps the sail stay up. When the sail catches the wind, the wind fills up the sail. The force of the wind pushes the boat forward. If the wind does not blow, the boat will not move. This is why a **marine engineer**, or a person who designs boats, pays close attention to how a sail is made. The cloth of a sail must be strong. The shape of a sail must help catch the wind. Lastly, a sail must be the right size. A small sail will not catch the wind. A sail that is too big and heavy will tip the boat over.

STEM Challenge: Sailboat

Visual Literacy

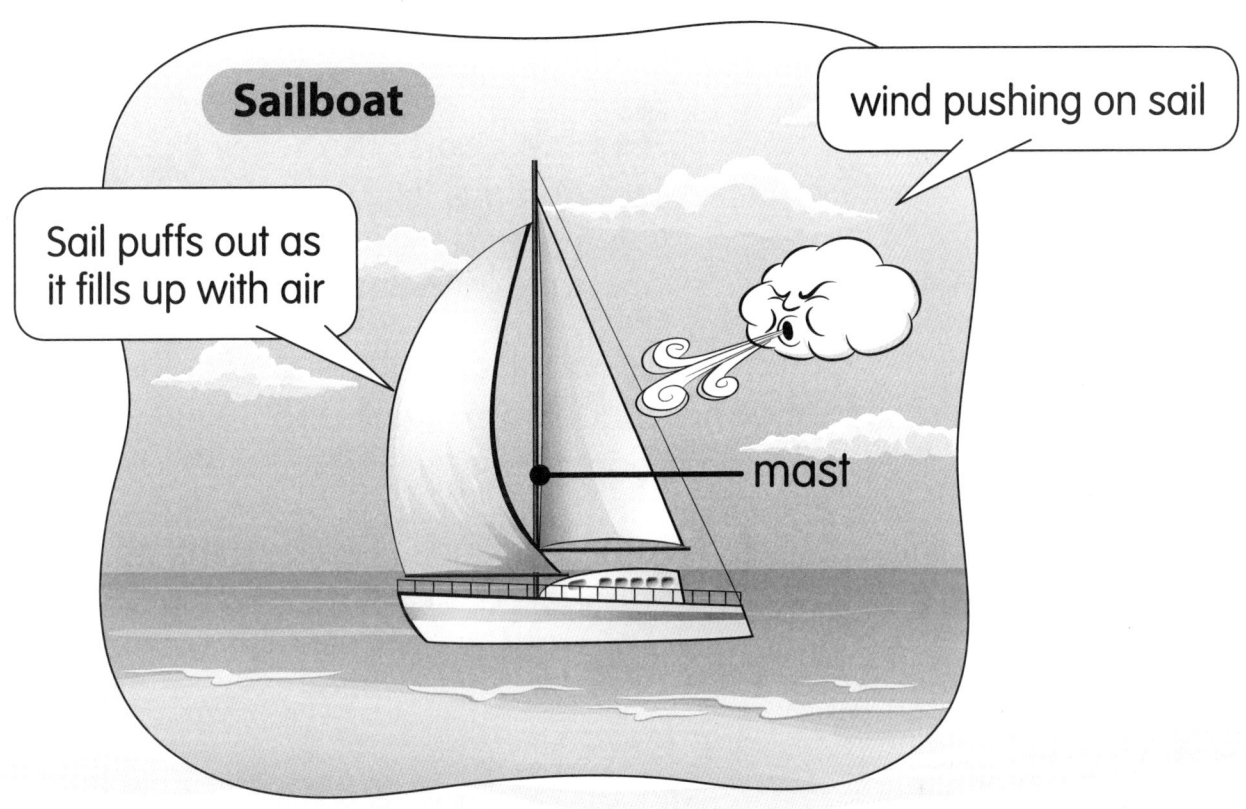

Sailboat

Sail puffs out as it fills up with air

wind pushing on sail

mast

Different Shapes of Sails

Physical Science 83

STEM Challenge: Sailboat

Sailboat

Challenge: Make a sail that uses wind power to move a boat.

Testable goals: The sail will fit on a craft stick and help a toy boat travel forward 2 feet (60 centimeters).

Research: Look at pictures of sailboats. Notice the shape of the sails and the materials they are made from. Think about how sails use wind power to move a boat.

Brainstorm: Think about all the different kinds of sails. Think about the sail you want to make. Then draw a picture of it in the box.

STEM Challenge: Sailboat

Suggested Materials List

Items for each group

- ☐ glue
- ☐ tape
- ☐ scissors
- ☐ craft stick

- ☐ **boat:** Provide each group with 1 foam block at least 2 inches (5 centimeters) thick, with a slit for a craft stick in the middle.

Items for the whole class

- ☐ aluminum foil
- ☐ paper
- ☐ tissue paper
- ☐ wax paper
- ☐ plastic bags
- ☐ index cards
- ☐ felt

- ☐ paper cups
- ☐ straws
- ☐ craft sticks
- ☐ _____
- ☐ _____
- ☐ _____
- ☐ _____

Items for testing

- ☐ fan or straws to make wind
- ☐ large tub or sink of water

- ☐ ruler or tape measure
- ☐ boat

STEM Challenge: Sailboat

Think About the Design Process

Plan
Think about the things you have. How can you use them to make a sail that helps a boat move?

Create
Look at the design you drew. Then use the things you have to make a sail.

Test
Place your sail on the boat. Place your boat in the tub or sink of water. Turn on the fan or blow through a straw. Does your boat move? Does it move 2 feet (60 centimeters)? Does your sail stay on the boat? Does the boat tip over?

How Did It Work?
Think about what happened when you tested your sail. Did your design work? What can you do to make it better?

Plan, create, and test until you are happy with your sail.

STEM Challenge: Sailboat

Design Process

 **Plan:** Write about your design. Tell what things you will use. Then draw your design.

 **Create**

 **Test:** Write about or draw to show what happened when you did your tests.

 **How Did It Work?** Write what you think.

STEM Challenge: Sailboat

Redesign Process

 **Redesign:** Write about what you will change. Draw your new design.

 **Change It or Make It Again**

 **Test:** Write about or draw to show what happened when you did your tests.

 **How Did It Work?** Write what you think.

STEM Challenge: Play Structures

Task: Students will work in small groups to design a play structure that uses a push or pull.

Getting Started

Build Content Knowledge
If you wish to provide students with background knowledge about force and motion, reproduce and distribute pages 90 and 91. Preview the Visual Literacy page with students. Then read the Science Concept page to students as they follow along, or, if they are able, have them read it independently. Next, discuss the science concept and the visual literacy graphics on those pages.

Introduce the Challenge
Reproduce and distribute the STEM Challenge on page 92. Then have students read the challenge and the testable goals. Discuss the materials with the students and decide on a plan for gathering the materials.

Next help students research different structures on the playground. Ask them to think about how science, technology, engineering, and math can be used to create a play structure that uses a push or pull. Finally, have students independently brainstorm and draw their ideas on page 92.

Completing the Challenge

Assign students to small groups.

Optional: Model the Design Process
You may wish to reproduce and distribute page 94 to students. This resource is intended to help students think about how to approach each step in the design process.

Design Process Worksheets
Reproduce and distribute the STEM design process worksheets to students. Provide support when needed to help students describe and evaluate their plans.

After the Challenge
Have students share their design processes, compare their play structures, and brainstorm ideas for improvements.

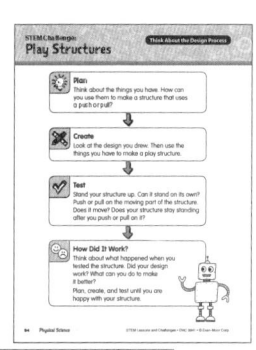

STEM Challenge: Play Structures

Science Concept

Forces on the Playground

Playgrounds have swings, slides, and merry-go-rounds. These are called **play structures**. Children slide down a slide, swing on a swing, and climb up the jungle gym. You use force when you do all these things.

Force is a push or pull. A **push** is when you move something away from you. You can push a shopping cart in a store. You can push a ball. You can push the merry-go-round on the playground.

A **pull** is when you move an object toward you. You can pull a dog on a leash. You can pull toys in a wagon. You can also pull on the bars of a ladder to climb a play structure. Your body or something moves because you are using force.

Pushes and pulls cause things to move. When something is moving, it is in **motion**. Things can move in many different ways. Some things can roll, spin, bounce, and slide. For example, a toy car that is sitting still is not in motion. To make it move, you need to put force on it. When you push the toy car, it starts to move. The toy car is now rolling and in motion.

STEM Challenge: Play Structures

Visual Literacy

A force is a push or pull.

Using Force on Playground Structures

Pushing the merry-go-round puts it in motion.

A girl pulls on the rope to climb.

STEM Challenge: Play Structures

Challenge

Play Structures

Challenge: Design a play structure that uses a push or pull.

Testable goals: The structure will have a moving part that can be pushed or pulled. The structure will stand on its own.

Research: Look at pictures of playground structures. Think about what type of force is needed to play on the structure.

Brainstorm: Think about all the different ways a play structure can look. Think about the play structure you will build. Then draw a picture of it in the box.

92 Physical Science

STEM Challenge: Play Structures

Suggested Materials List

Items for each group

- [ ] glue
- [ ] tape
- [ ] scissors

Items for the whole class

- [ ] straws
- [ ] craft sticks
- [ ] toothpicks
- [ ] unsharpened pencils
- [ ] pipe cleaners
- [ ] paper
- [ ] cardboard
- [ ] paper cups
- [ ] paper plates
- [ ] paper towel rolls
- [ ] aluminum foil
- [ ] construction paper
- [ ] paper clips
- [ ] spools
- [ ] wagon wheels or penne pasta (uncooked)
- [ ] lifesaver-shaped candy
- [ ] _____
- [ ] _____
- [ ] _____
- [ ] _____
- [ ] _____
- [ ] _____
- [ ] _____
- [ ] _____
- [ ] _____
- [ ] _____

STEM Challenge: Play Structures

Think About the Design Process

 ### Plan
Think about the things you have. How can you use them to make a structure that uses a push or pull?

 ### Create
Look at the design you drew. Then use the things you have to make a play structure.

 ### Test
Stand your structure up. Can it stand on its own? Push or pull on the moving part of the structure. Does it move? Does your structure stay standing after you push or pull it?

 ### How Did It Work?
Think about what happened when you tested the structure. Did your design work? What can you do to make it better?

Plan, create, and test until you are happy with your structure.

STEM Challenge: Play Structures

Design Process

 **Plan:** Write about your design. Tell what things you will use. Then draw your design.

 **Create**

 **Test:** Write about or draw to show what happened when you did your tests.

 **How Did It Work?** Write what you think.

STEM Challenge: Play Structures

Redesign Process

Redesign: Write about what you will change. Draw your new design.

Change It or Make It Again

Test: Write about or draw to show what happened when you did your tests.

How Did It Work? Write what you think.

STEM Challenge: Bird Feeder

Task: Students will work in small groups to design a bird feeder that will feed local birds in the winter.

Getting Started

Build Content Knowledge
If you wish to provide students with background knowledge about birds' feeding habits, reproduce and distribute pages 98 and 99. Preview the Visual Literacy page with students. Then read the Science Concept page to students as they follow along, or, if they are able, have them read it independently. Next, discuss the science concept and the visual literacy graphics on those pages.

Introduce the Challenge
Reproduce and distribute the STEM Challenge on page 100. Then have students read the challenge and the testable goals. Discuss the materials with the students and decide on a plan for gathering the materials.

Next help students research different birds that live around your school. Ask them to think about how science, technology, engineering, and math can be used to create a bird feeder. Finally, have students independently brainstorm and draw their ideas on page 100.

Completing the Challenge

Assign students to small groups.

Optional: Model the Design Process
You may wish to reproduce and distribute page 102 to students. This resource is intended to help students think about how to approach each step in the design process.

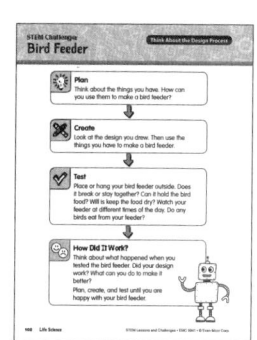

Design Process Worksheets
Reproduce and distribute the STEM design process worksheets to students. Provide support when needed to help students describe and evaluate their plans.

After the Challenge
Have students share their design processes, compare their bird feeders, and brainstorm ideas for improvements.

STEM Challenge: Bird Feeder

Science Concept

Eating in the Winter

All living things need food and shelter to live and grow. But in the winter, it can be hard for birds and other living things to find food. People make bird feeders to help birds find food easily. Before they make the feeder, they find out what birds live around them. They also find out what birds eat. Lastly, people think about the weather in their area.

A bird feeder is something that holds food for birds. Different birds eat different foods. We know what a bird eats by the shape of its beak. A hummingbird is a small bird. It has a long, thin beak to sip nectar from flowers. A songbird has a short, hard beak. This beak is good for picking up seeds and cracking nuts. A woodpecker has a long, hard beak. It pokes holes in trees and digs out the insects that live inside.

A bird feeder also gives shelter to birds. In some places around the world, it rains or snows. A bird feeder with a roof or cover keeps the birds and bird food dry. Some bird feeders also have a place for birds to stand while they eat. The feeders can be hung in a tree or placed on the ground.

STEM Challenge: Bird Feeder

Visual Literacy

This bird feeder is filled with sugar water. It has small holes for the beaks of hummingbirds. It also has a bar for the birds to stand on while they eat.

Woodpeckers love to eat insects. This woodpecker is eating balls made from fruit, seeds, and insects.

The roofs on the feeders keep the food dry when it rains or snows. The open sides let all birds, with big beaks and small beaks, eat from the feeder.

STEM Challenge: Bird Feeder

Challenge

Bird Feeder

Challenge: Design a bird feeder that will hold food for birds during the winter.

Testable goals: The bird feeder will hold food, keep it dry, and feed birds.

Research: Look at pictures of different birds that live around your school. Notice the shape of their beaks. Find out what the birds like to eat. Think about the weather around your school during the wintertime.

Brainstorm: Think about what a bird's beak looks like. Think about the bird feeder you want to make. Then draw a picture of it in the box.

STEM Challenge: Bird Feeder

Suggested Materials List

Items for each group

- ☐ glue
- ☐ tape
- ☐ scissors

Items for the whole class

- ☐ empty plastic water bottles
- ☐ empty milk cartons
- ☐ empty tissue boxes
- ☐ egg cartons
- ☐ paper plates
- ☐ paper cups
- ☐ cardboard
- ☐ construction paper
- ☐ aluminum foil
- ☐ craft sticks
- ☐ straws
- ☐ pipe cleaners
- ☐ string
- ☐ _____
- ☐ _____
- ☐ _____

Items for testing

- ☐ food that local birds will eat
  (fruit, seeds, insects, sugar water, etc.)

Life Science

STEM Challenge: Bird Feeder

Think About the Design Process

Plan
Think about the things you have. How can you use them to make a bird feeder?

Create
Look at the design you drew. Then use the things you have to make a bird feeder.

Test
Place or hang your bird feeder outside. Does it break or stay together? Can it hold the bird food? Will it keep the food dry? Watch your feeder at different times of the day. Do any birds eat from your feeder?

How Did It Work?
Think about what happened when you tested the bird feeder. Did your design work? What can you do to make it better?

Plan, create, and test until you are happy with your bird feeder.

STEM Challenge: Bird Feeder

Design Process

 **Plan:** Write about your design. Tell what things you will use. Then draw your design.

 **Create**

 **Test:** Write about or draw to show what happened when you did your tests.

 **How Did It Work?** Write what you think.

STEM Challenge: Bird Feeder

Redesign Process

 **Redesign:** Write about what you will change. Draw your new design.

 **Change It or Make It Again**

 **Test:** Write about or draw to show what happened when you did your tests.

 **How Did It Work?** Write what you think.

STEM Challenge: Insect Catcher

Task: Students will work in small groups to design a device that will safely catch an insect.

Getting Started

Build Content Knowledge
If you wish to provide students with background knowledge about how scientists study insects, reproduce and distribute pages 106 and 107. Preview the Visual Literacy page with students. Then read the Science Concept page to students as they follow along, or, if they are able, have them read it independently. Next, discuss the science concept and the visual literacy graphics on those pages.

Introduce the Challenge
Reproduce and distribute the STEM Challenge on page 108. Then have students read the challenge and the testable goals. Discuss the materials with the students and decide on a plan for gathering the materials.

Next help students research different insects around your school. Ask them to think about how science, technology, engineering, and math can be used to create a device that will catch an insect. Finally, have students independently brainstorm and draw their ideas on page 108.

Completing the Challenge

Assign students to small groups.

Optional: Model the Design Process
You may wish to reproduce and distribute page 110 to students. This resource is intended to help students think about how to approach each step in the design process.

Design Process Worksheets
Reproduce and distribute the STEM design process worksheets to students. Provide support when needed to help students describe and evaluate their plans.

After the Challenge
Have students share their design processes, compare their insect catchers, and brainstorm ideas for improvements.

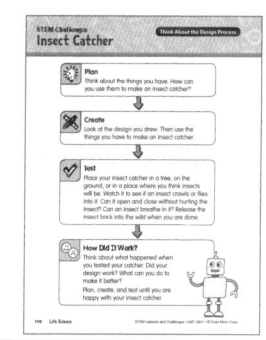

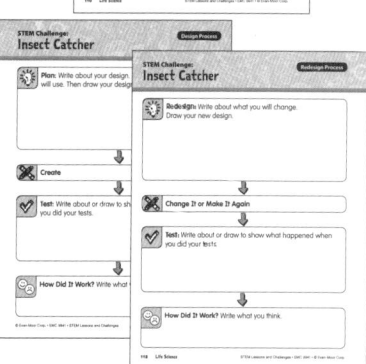

STEM Challenge: Insect Catcher

Studying Insects

Insects are the largest group of animals on Earth. Scientists catch insects and study them. They learn how insects live and grow. They learn how they help our world. Scientists know of a million different types of insects. But they believe there are still many they do not know about.

Scientists find insects in different places. Some insects can be found in the dirt. Many insects can be found on plants or in the grass. Other insects fly by plants and bodies of water.

There are different ways scientists catch insects. Scientists use things that insects like. Some insects like bright colors. Most insects like to eat food. Insects eat juicy leaves, sweet candy, and even rotting food. But scientists make sure they do not hurt the insects. They put them back into nature after they study them.

Some people think insects are pests. But many insects do important things. This is why scientists study them. Insects help keep Earth healthy. People and animals need insects so they can live on Earth.

STEM Challenge: Insect Catcher

Visual Literacy

Scientists Study Insects

Where to Find Insects

  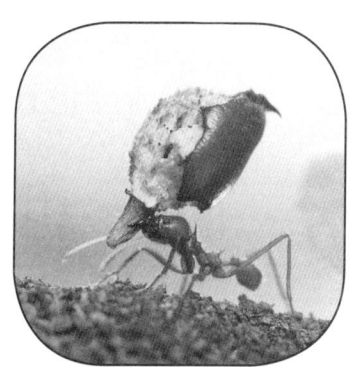

Flying near water · On plants · In the dirt

What Insects Like

A beetle eating a rotten banana · A grasshopper eating a leaf · Ants eating a sweet lollipop

STEM Challenge: Insect Catcher

Insect Catcher

Challenge: Create an insect catcher that will safely catch an insect.

Testable goals: The insect catcher will open and close. It will keep the insect safe. It will not hurt the insect.

Research: Look at insects that live around your school. Notice where they can be found. Think about how the insects move and what they like to eat.

Brainstorm: Think about how different things that catch insects look. Think about the insect catcher that you want to build. Then draw a picture of it in the box.

STEM Challenge: Insect Catcher

Suggested Materials List

Items for each group

- ☐ glue
- ☐ tape
- ☐ scissors

Items for the whole class

- ☐ cardboard
- ☐ paper towel rolls
- ☐ paper plates
- ☐ construction paper
- ☐ plastic cups
- ☐ egg cartons
- ☐ craft sticks
- ☐ pipe cleaners
- ☐ straws
- ☐ mesh netting
- ☐ paper clips
- ☐ rubber bands
- ☐ string
- ☐ _____

Items for testing

- ☐ food items (candy, marshmallows, fruit, etc.)
- ☐ items from nature (grass, leaves, flowers, sticks, etc.)

STEM Challenge: Insect Catcher

Think About the Design Process

Plan
Think about the things you have. How can you use them to make an insect catcher?

Create
Look at the design you drew. Then use the things you have to make an insect catcher.

Test
Place your insect catcher in a tree, on the ground, or in a place where you think insects will be. Watch it to see if an insect crawls or flies into it. Can it open and close without hurting the insect? Can an insect breathe in it? Release the insect back into the wild when you are done.

How Did It Work?
Think about what happened when you tested your catcher. Did your design work? What can you do to make it better?

Plan, create, and test until you are happy with your insect catcher.

STEM Challenge: Insect Catcher

Design Process

 **Plan:** Write about your design. Tell what things you will use. Then draw your design.

 **Create**

 **Test:** Write about or draw to show what happened when you did your tests.

 **How Did It Work?** Write what you think.

STEM Challenge: Insect Catcher

Redesign Process

 **Redesign:** Write about what you will change. Draw your new design.

 **Change It or Make It Again**

 **Test:** Write about or draw to show what happened when you did your tests.

 **How Did It Work?** Write what you think.

STEM Challenge: Joey Pouch

Task: Students will work in small groups to design a pouch that will carry a stuffed animal.

Getting Started

Build Content Knowledge
If you wish to provide students with background knowledge about kangaroos and their pouches, reproduce and distribute pages 114 and 115. Preview the Visual Literacy page with students. Then read the Science Concept page to students as they follow along, or, if they are able, have them read it independently. Next, discuss the science concept and the visual literacy graphics on those pages.

Introduce the Challenge
Reproduce and distribute the STEM Challenge on page 116. Then have students read the challenge and the testable goals. Discuss the materials with the students and decide on a plan for gathering the materials.

Next help students research how kangaroos use their pouches. Ask them to think about how science, technology, engineering, and math can be used to create a pouch for a stuffed animal. Finally, have students independently brainstorm and draw their ideas on page 116.

Completing the Challenge

Assign students to small groups.

Optional: Model the Design Process
You may wish to reproduce and distribute page 118 to students. This resource is intended to help students think about how to approach each step in the design process.

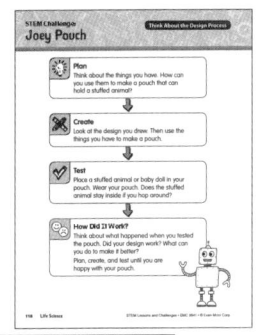

Design Process Worksheets
Reproduce and distribute the STEM design process worksheets to students. Provide support when needed to help students describe and evaluate their plans.

After the Challenge
Have students share their design processes, compare their pouches, and brainstorm ideas for improvements.

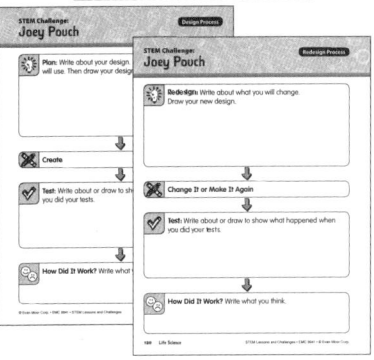

STEM Challenge: Joey Pouch

Science Concept

A Safe Place for a Joey

Animals have body parts that help their babies survive. For kangaroos, their pouches help their babies live and grow. Kangaroos are mammals that have two powerful back legs and big feet. They also have a long, strong tail and two small front legs. They live in Australia. Kangaroos have many important body parts. But kangaroos are most known for their pouches.

A kangaroo pouch is a big pocket made out of skin. Only female kangaroos have a pouch on their bellies. They use it to hold their babies, called **joeys**. The pouch can stretch wide to allow joeys to move in or out. When the joey is inside, the opening of the pouch closes snuggly so the joey will not fall out.

Joeys are born the size of a jelly bean. Mother kangaroos carry their joeys in their pouches. The pouch provides milk, warmth, and a safe place to live. A joey can live in its mother's pouch for up to 12 months. It will leave the pouch only when it is strong enough to survive outside of the pouch on its own.

STEM Challenge: Joey Pouch

Visual Literacy

A joey hopping around its mother

A joey climbing back inside its mother's pouch

A joey safe in its mother's pouch

STEM Challenge: Joey Pouch

Joey Pouch

Challenge: Make a pouch that can hold a stuffed animal.

Testable goals: A person can wear the pouch, it can open and close, and it can hold a stuffed animal.

Research: Look at pictures of kangaroos. Notice the pouch and where it is located. Think about what the pouch provides for a joey.

Brainstorm: Think about what kangaroos' pouches look like. Think about the pouch you want to make. Then draw a picture of it in the box.

STEM Challenge: Joey Pouch

Suggested Materials List

Items for each group

- [ ] scissors
- [ ] duct tape

Items for the whole class

- [ ] paper bag
- [ ] plastic bag
- [ ] netting
- [ ] old knit t-shirt
- [ ] rubber bands
- [ ] string
- [ ] _____
- [ ] _____
- [ ] _____
- [ ] _____
- [ ] _____
- [ ] _____

Item for testing

- [ ] stuffed animal

STEM Challenge: Joey Pouch

Think About the Design Process

Plan
Think about the things you have. How can you use them to make a pouch that can hold a stuffed animal?

Create
Look at the design you drew. Then use the things you have to make a pouch.

Test
Place a stuffed animal or baby doll in your pouch. Wear your pouch. Does the stuffed animal stay inside if you hop around?

How Did It Work?
Think about what happened when you tested the pouch. Did your design work? What can you do to make it better?

Plan, create, and test until you are happy with your pouch.

STEM Challenge: Joey Pouch

Design Process

 **Plan:** Write about your design. Tell what things you will use. Then draw your design.

 **Create**

 **Test:** Write about or draw to show what happened when you did your tests.

 **How Did It Work?** Write what you think.

STEM Challenge: Joey Pouch

Redesign Process

 **Redesign:** Write about what you will change. Draw your new design.

 **Change It or Make It Again**

 **Test:** Write about or draw to show what happened when you did your tests.

 **How Did It Work?** Write what you think.

STEM Challenge: Tool from Nature

Task: Students will work in small groups to design a tool that works like a crab claw.

Getting Started

Build Content Knowledge
If you wish to provide students with background knowledge about biomimicry, reproduce and distribute pages 122 and 123. Preview the Visual Literacy page with students. Then read the Science Concept page to students as they follow along, or, if they are able, have them read it independently. Next, discuss the science concept and the visual literacy graphics on those pages.

Introduce the Challenge
Reproduce and distribute the STEM Challenge on page 124. Then have students read the challenge and the testable goal. Discuss the materials with the students and decide on a plan for gathering the materials.

Next help students research crabs and how they use their claws. Ask them to think about how science, technology, engineering, and math can be used to create a tool that works like a crab claw. Finally, have students independently brainstorm and draw their ideas on page 124.

Completing the Challenge

Assign students to small groups.

Optional: Model the Design Process
You may wish to reproduce and distribute page 126 to students. This resource is intended to help students think about how to approach each step in the design process.

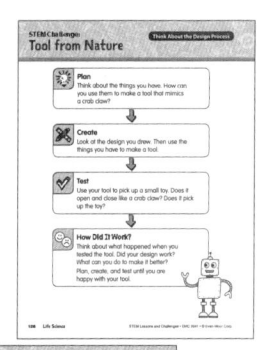

Design Process Worksheets
Reproduce and distribute the STEM design process worksheets to students. Provide support when needed to help students describe and evaluate their plans.

After the Challenge
Have students share their design processes, compare their tools, and brainstorm ideas for improvements.

STEM Challenge: Tool from Nature

Science Concept

Learning from Nature

Engineers can learn by looking at nature. Nature is everything in our world that is not made by people. Plants and animals are from nature. Engineers use something called **biomimicry** to learn from nature. That means they look at how things work in the natural world, and they **mimic**, or copy, those things to solve problems.

For example, when a person falls off a bike, he or she may get hurt. To solve this problem, engineers looked at turtle shells. Turtle shells are hard and do not break easily. The hard shell helps keep the turtle's soft body safe. Engineers copied turtle shells and made a tool called a helmet.

Other things were made by looking at animals. Airplanes were made to look and act like the wings of a bird.

Plants also help engineers solve problems. A barbed wire fence was made to be like the sharp thorns on a bush. A barbed wire fence helps keep animals in or out of an area. Looking at plants and animals can help people solve many problems.

STEM Challenge: Tool from Nature

Visual Literacy

Thorn bush from nature

Barbed wire made by people

Turtle from nature

Helmet made by people

Bird from nature

Airplane made by people

STEM Challenge: Tool from Nature

Tool from Nature

Challenge: Make a tool that mimics a crab claw.

Testable goal: The tool will pick up a small toy.

Research: Look at pictures or videos of how crabs use their claws. Notice how the claws are shaped and where they are on the crab's body.

Brainstorm: Think about how a crab's claw looks and works. Think about the tool you want to make. Then draw a picture of it in the box.

124 Life Science

STEM Challenge: Tool from Nature

Suggested Materials List

Items for each group

- ☐ glue
- ☐ tape
- ☐ scissors

Items for the whole class

- ☐ cardboard
- ☐ paper
- ☐ aluminum foil
- ☐ paper cups
- ☐ craft sticks
- ☐ straws
- ☐ pipe cleaners
- ☐ paper clips
- ☐ fasteners
- ☐ _____
- ☐ _____
- ☐ _____
- ☐ _____
- ☐ _____

Item for testing

- ☐ small toy

STEM Challenge: Tool from Nature

Think About the Design Process

Plan
Think about the things you have. How can you use them to make a tool that mimics a crab claw?

Create
Look at the design you drew. Then use the things you have to make a tool.

Test
Use your tool to pick up a small toy. Does it open and close like a crab claw? Does it pick up the toy?

How Did It Work?
Think about what happened when you tested the tool. Did your design work? What can you do to make it better?

Plan, create, and test until you are happy with your tool.

STEM Challenge: Tool from Nature

Design Process

 **Plan:** Write about your design. Tell what things you will use. Then draw your design.

 **Create**

 **Test:** Write about or draw to show what happened when you did your tests.

 **How Did It Work?** Write what you think.

STEM Challenge: Tool from Nature

Redesign Process

 **Redesign:** Write about what you will change. Draw your new design.

 **Change It or Make It Again**

 **Test:** Write about or draw to show what happened when you did your tests.

 **How Did It Work?** Write what you think.